CREATIVE KEYBOARD PRESENTS

KID'S ELECTRONIC KEYBOARD M

BY WILLIAM BAY

Power Switch

Before we can begin, turn on your keyboard.

OFF ON

Power

Voicings

Your keyboard can sound like many different instruments. Yours may be able to sound like a flute, piano, organ, trumpet, harpsichord, or many other instruments. Play any key and try out the different sounds. Which ones do you like?

1 2 3 4 5 6 7 8 9 0

Correct Position

1. Sit comfortably and lean slightly forward.
2. Relax arms and shoulders.
3. Put feet flat on the floor.

1. Fingers should be slightly arched or rounded.
2. Play with tips of fingers.
3. Play with the side of tip of the thumb.

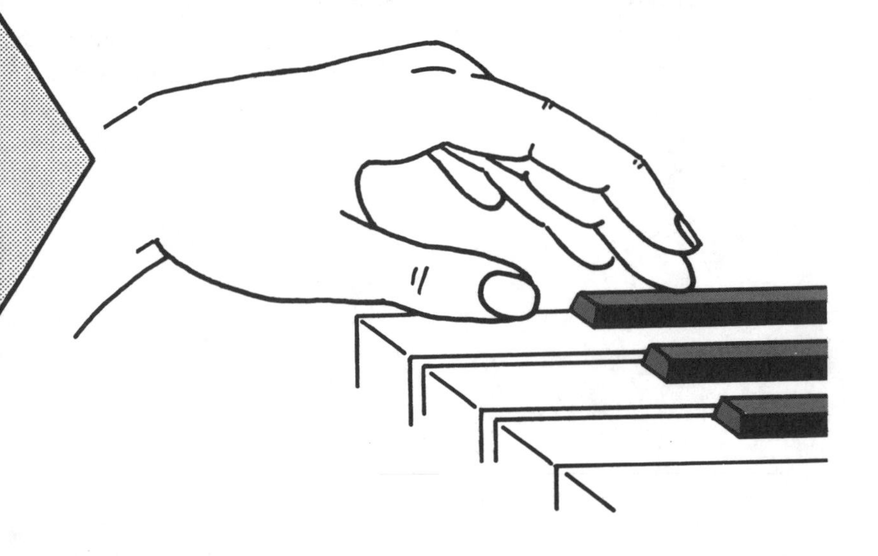

Types of Notes & Rests

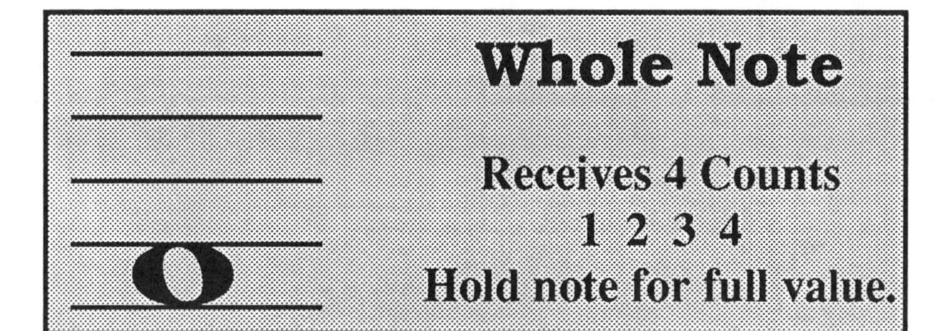

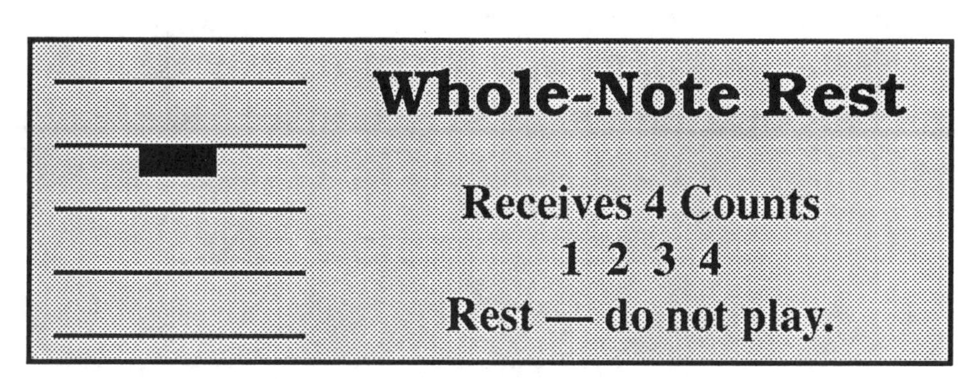

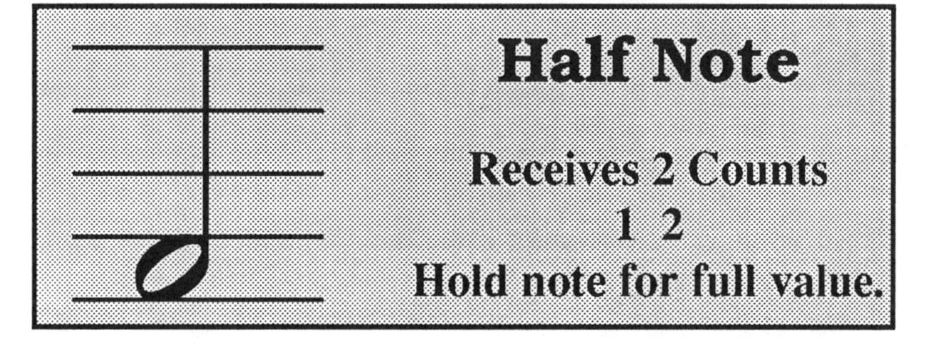

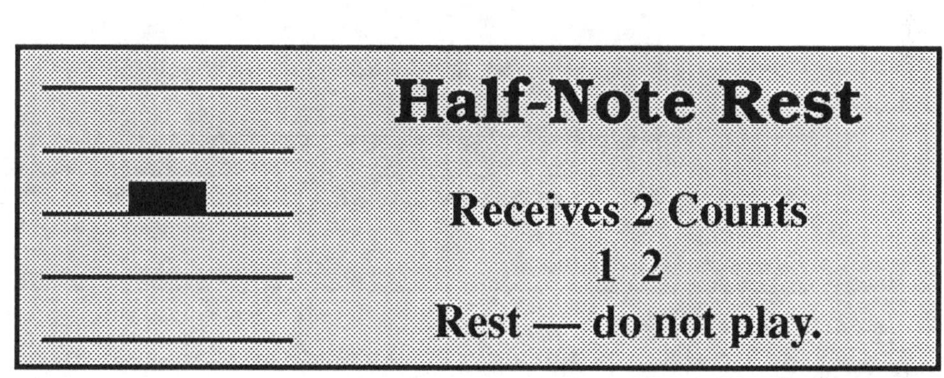

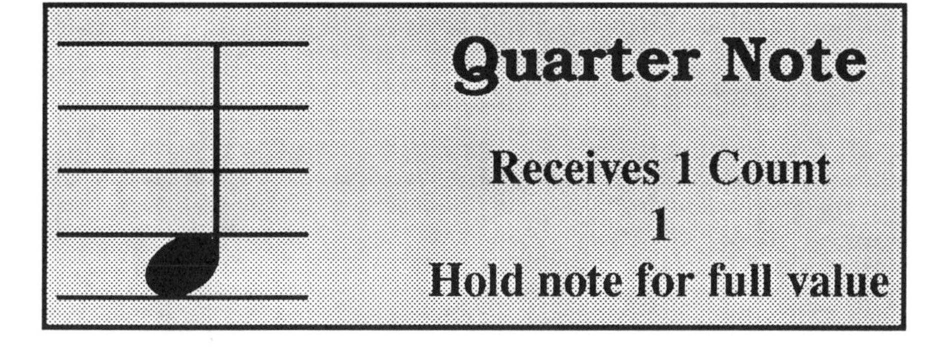

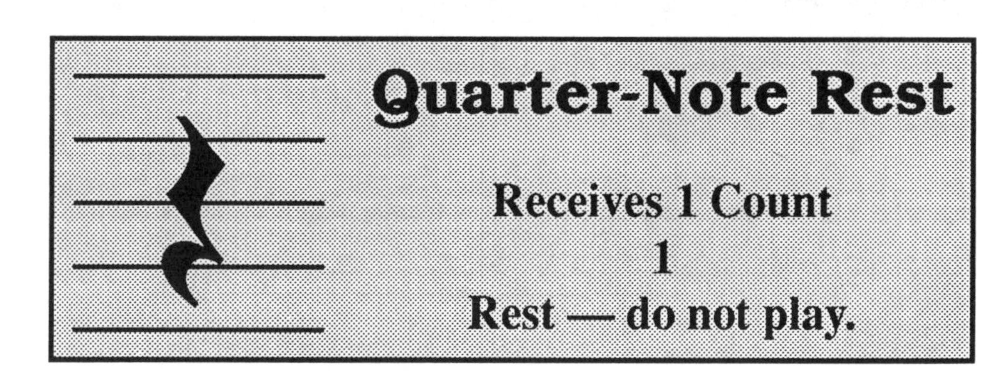

Time Signatures

At the beginning of a song, you will see a time signature. This number will tell you how many beats are to be played in a measure of music.

3
4

Count 3 Beats Per Measure

Example: 1 2 3, 1 2 3, 1 2 3, etc.

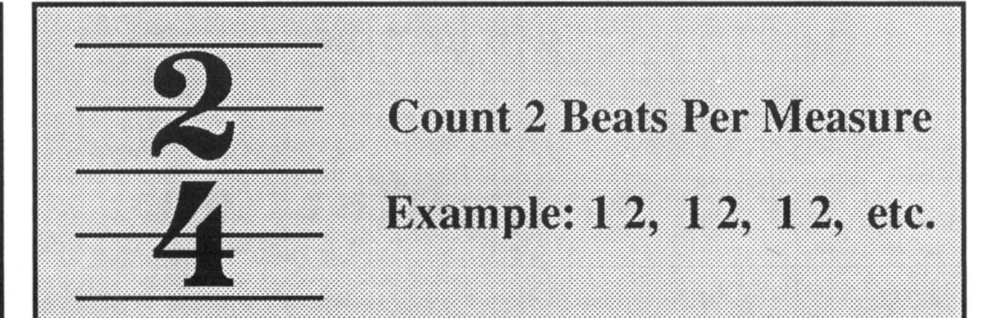

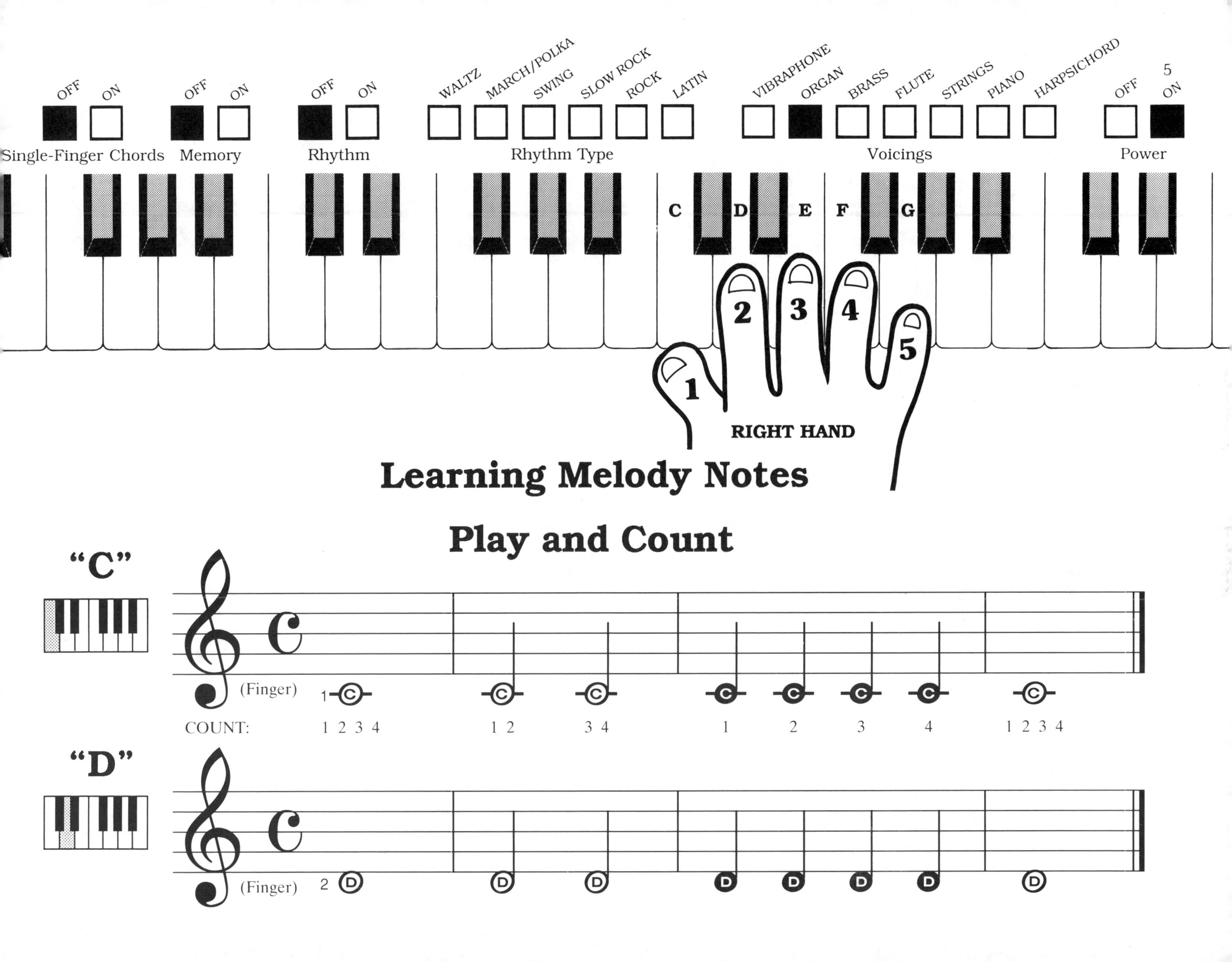
OFF
ON
OFF
ON
OFF
ON
WALTZ
MARCH/POLKA
SWING
SLOW ROCK
ROCK
LATIN
VIBRAPHONE
ORGAN
BRASS
FLUTE
STRINGS
PIANO
HARPSICHORD
OFF
5
ON
Single-Finger Chords
Memory
Rhythm
Rhythm Type
Voicings
Power
C
D
E
F
G
1
2
3
4
5
RIGHT HAND
Learning Melody Notes
Play and Count
"C"
(Finger)
1
COUNT:
1 2 3 4
1 2
3 4
1
2
3
4
1 2 3 4
"D"
(Finger)
2

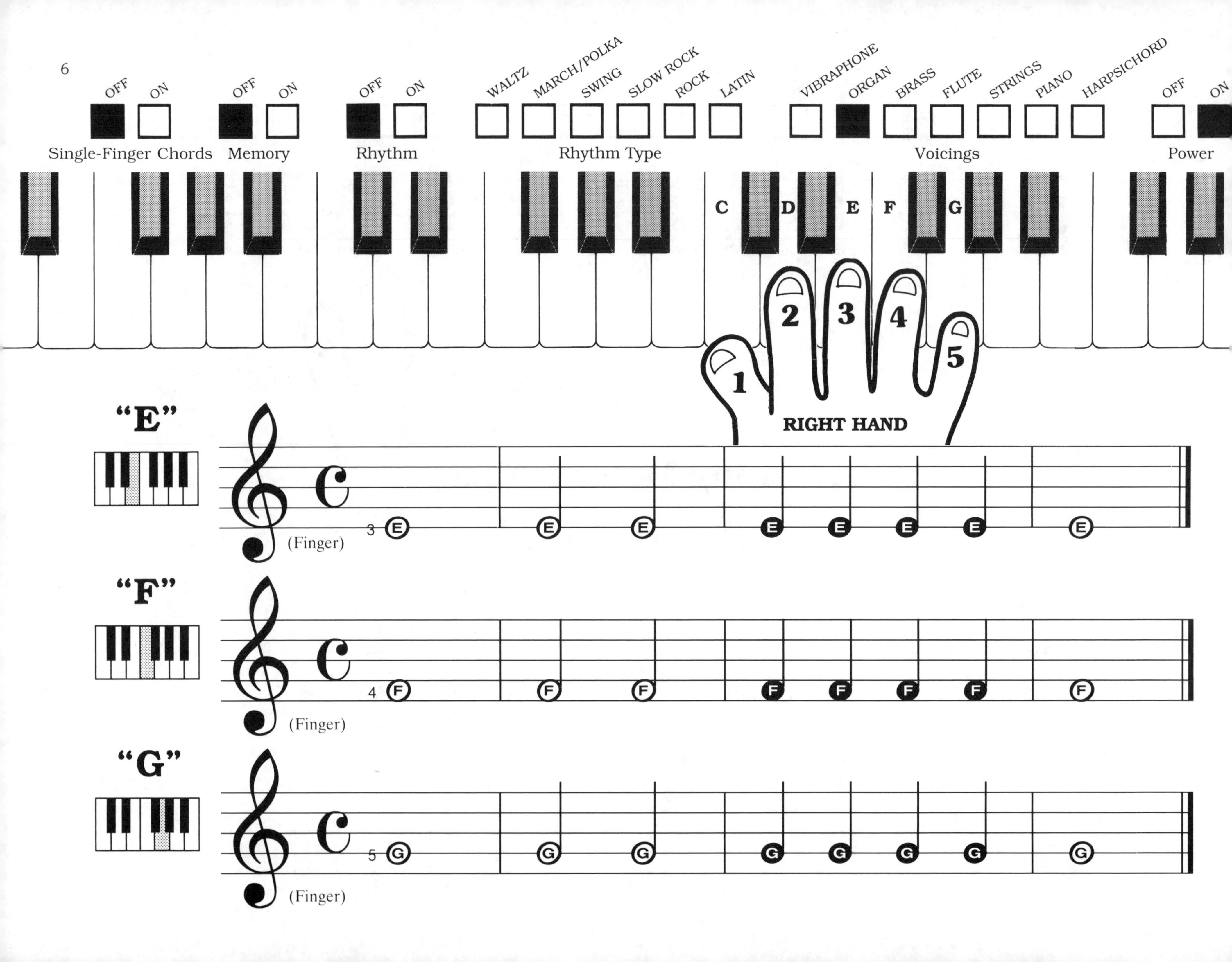
OFF
ON
OFF
ON
OFF
ON
WALTZ
MARCH/POLKA
SWING
SLOW ROCK
ROCK
LATIN
VIBRAPHONE
ORGAN
BRASS
FLUTE
STRINGS
PIANO
HARPSICHORD
OFF
ON
Single-Finger Chords
Memory
Rhythm
Rhythm Type
Voicings
Power
C
D
E
F
G
1
2
3
4
5
RIGHT HAND
"E"
3
(Finger)
E E E E E E E E
"F"
4
(Finger)
F F F F F F F F
"G"
5
(Finger)
G G G G G G G G

Rhythm

1. Your keyboard has many different kinds of rhythms. Some common ones are rock, slow rock, waltz, swing, Latin, tango, march, and polka. There can be many more. Turn on your keyboard and listen to how each rhythm sounds.

2. **Tempo** means how fast you are going to play a song. In this book, set the rhythm very slow on each piece at first. When you have learned the notes, then try it a little faster.

Mixup

Turn your rhythm on to "March or Polka" and try the new song on the next page.

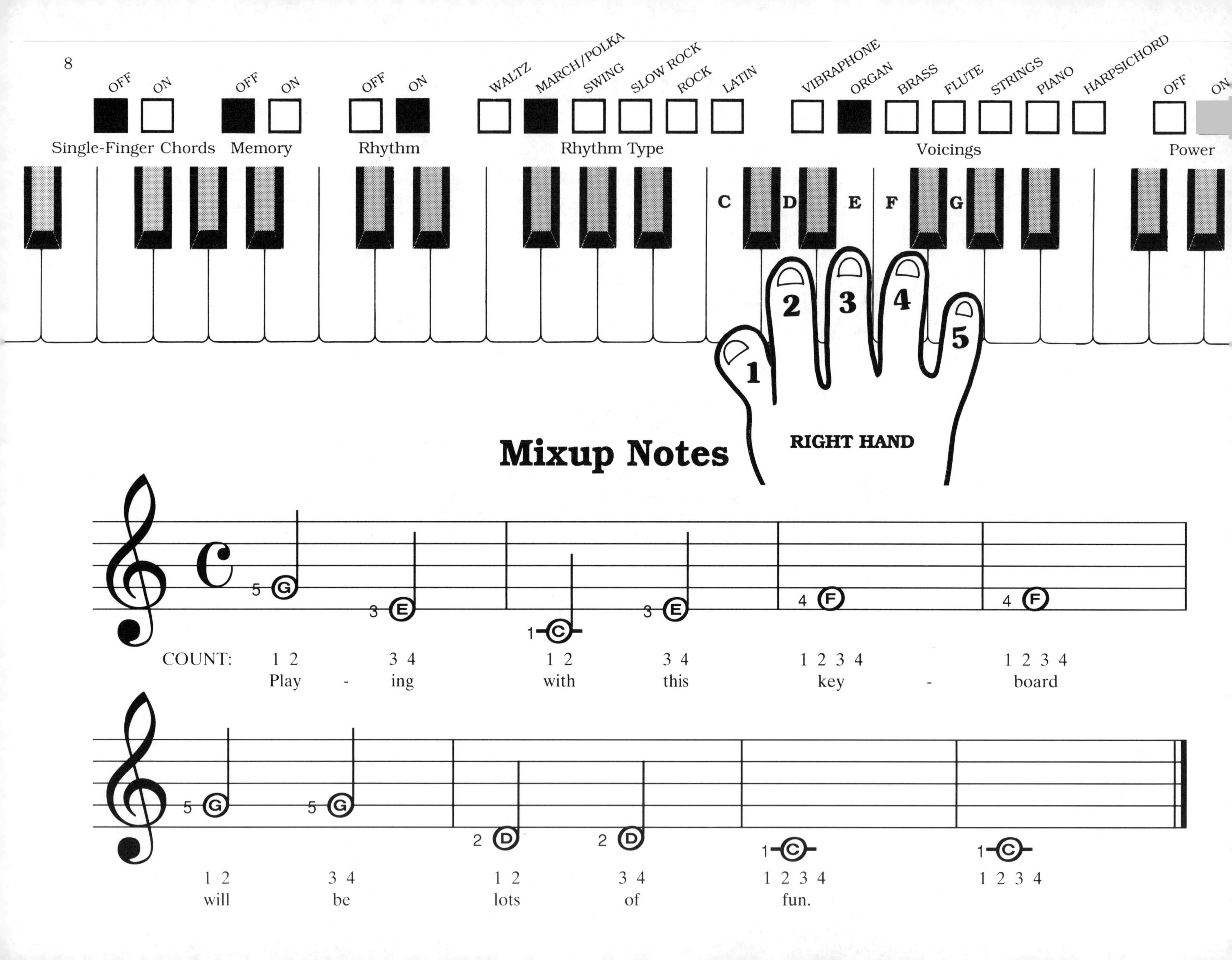
OFF
ON
Single-Finger Chords
OFF
ON
Memory
OFF
ON
Rhythm
WALTZ
MARCH/POLKA
SWING
SLOW ROCK
ROCK
LATIN
Rhythm Type
VIBRAPHONE
ORGAN
BRASS
FLUTE
STRINGS
PIANO
HARPSICHORD
Voicings
OFF
ON
Power
C
D
E
F
G
1
2
3
4
5
RIGHT HAND
Mixup Notes
5 G
3 E
1 C
3 E
4 F
4 F
COUNT: 1 2 3 4 1 2 3 4 1 2 3 4 1 2 3 4
Play - ing with this key - board
5 G
5 G
2 D
2 D
1 C
1 C
1 2 3 4 1 2 3 4 1 2 3 4 1 2 3 4
will be lots of fun.

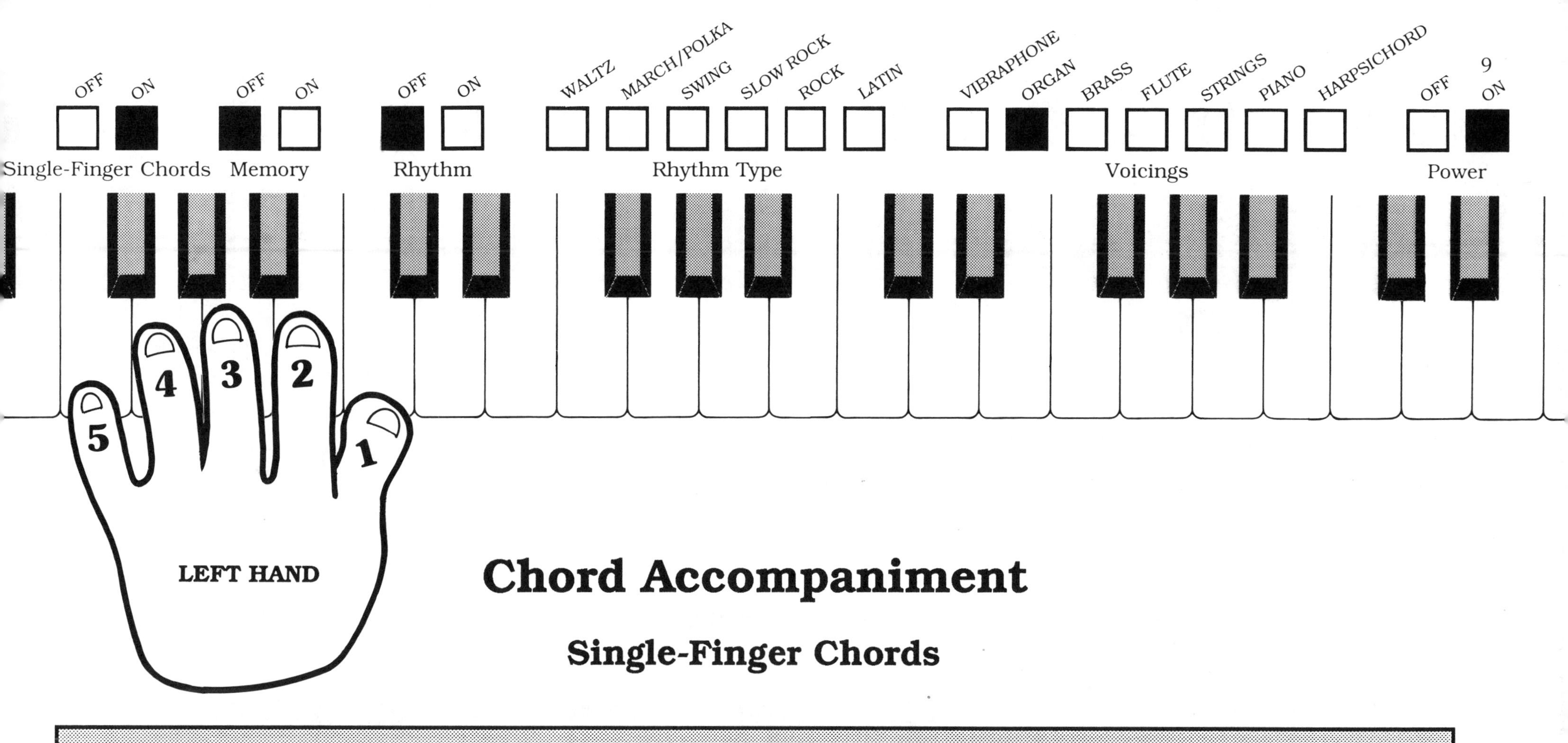

Chord Accompaniment

Single-Finger Chords

A chord is a grouping of 3 or more notes. We use chords to accompany the songs we play. Your keyboard will allow you to play chords with only 1 finger! Want to try this out? First place your left hand where shown on the diagram. Next, turn on the automatic chord switch (it may say "Single-Finger Chords" or something like that). Now play any key with your left hand and listen to how it sounds!

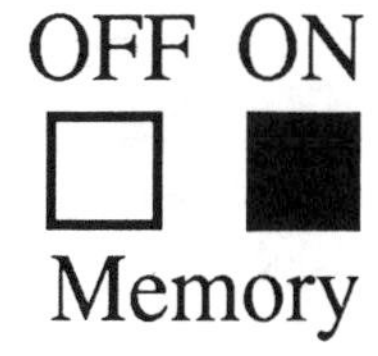

Your keyboard most likely has a "Memory" button or switch near the "Single-Finger Chords" button. When you turn this on and play a chord with your left hand, the chord will continue to sound until you play a new one! Try it.

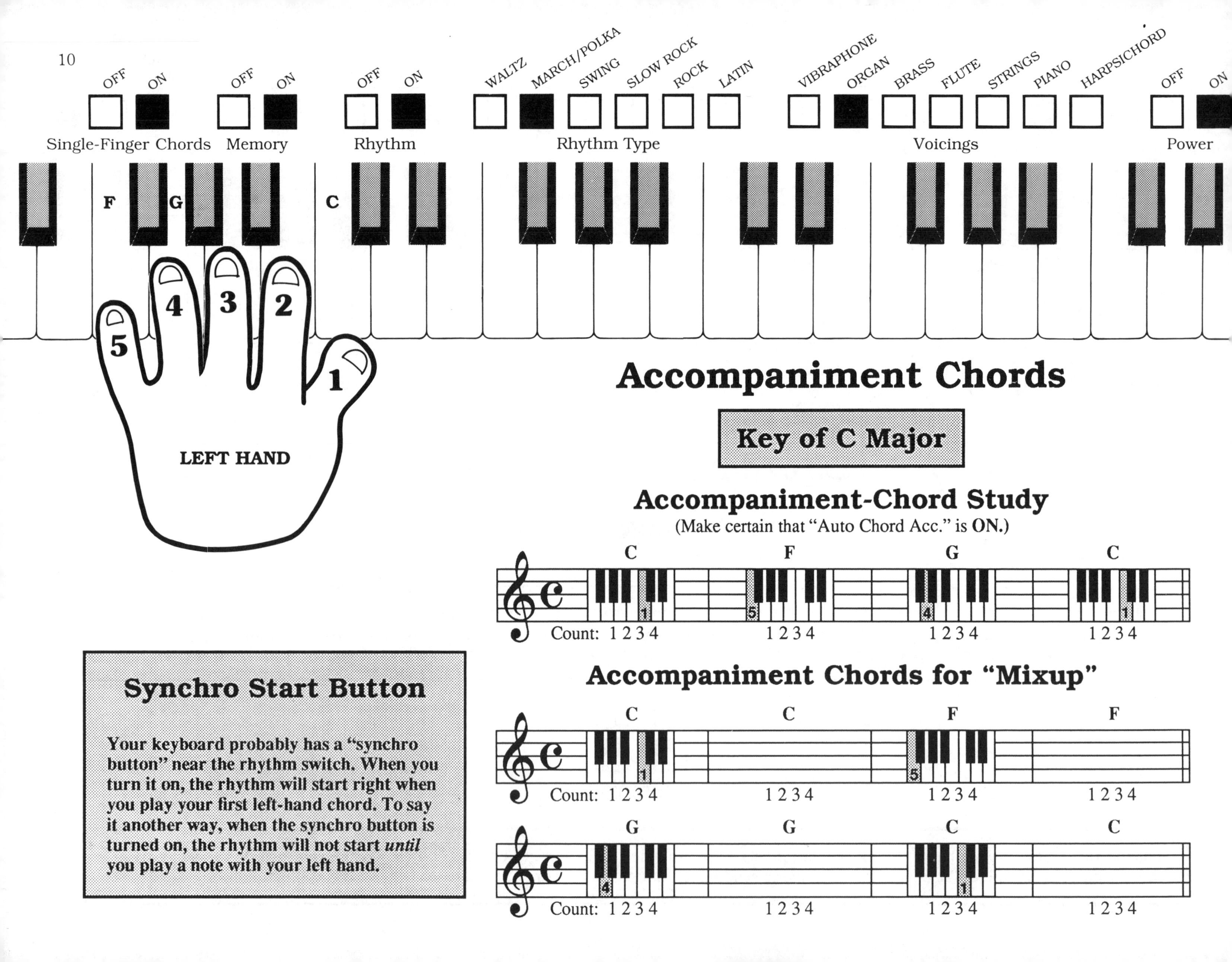

Accompaniment Chords

Key of C Major

Accompaniment-Chord Study

(Make certain that "Auto Chord Acc." is **ON.**)

Accompaniment Chords for "Mixup"

Synchro Start Button

Your keyboard probably has a "synchro button" near the rhythm switch. When you turn it on, the rhythm will start right when you play your first left-hand chord. To say it another way, when the synchro button is turned on, the rhythm will not start *until* you play a note with your left hand.

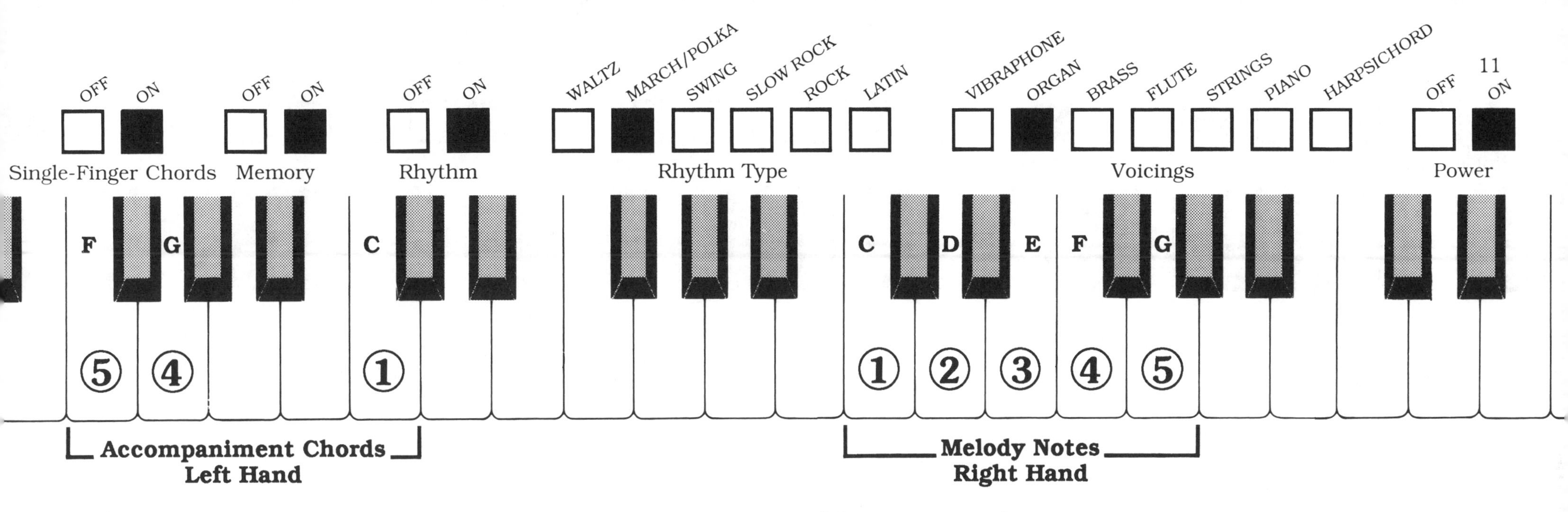

Mix-Up Notes All Together

Keyboard Song

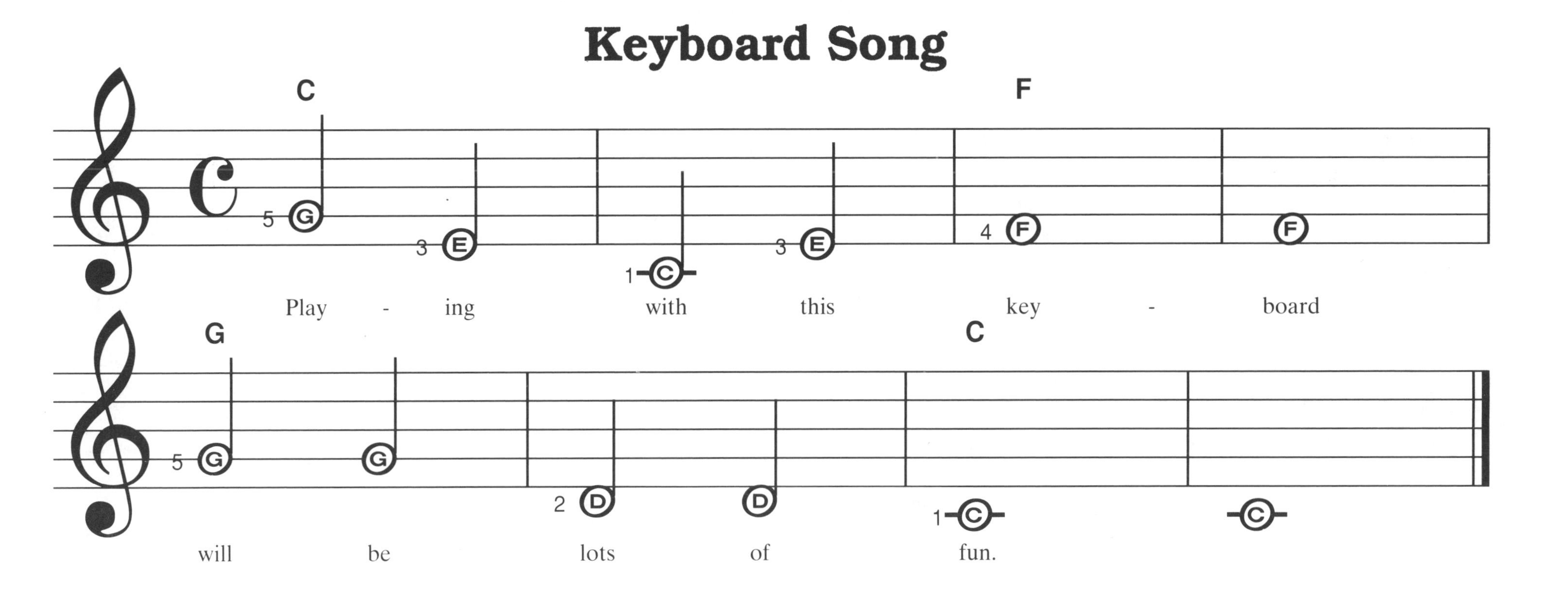

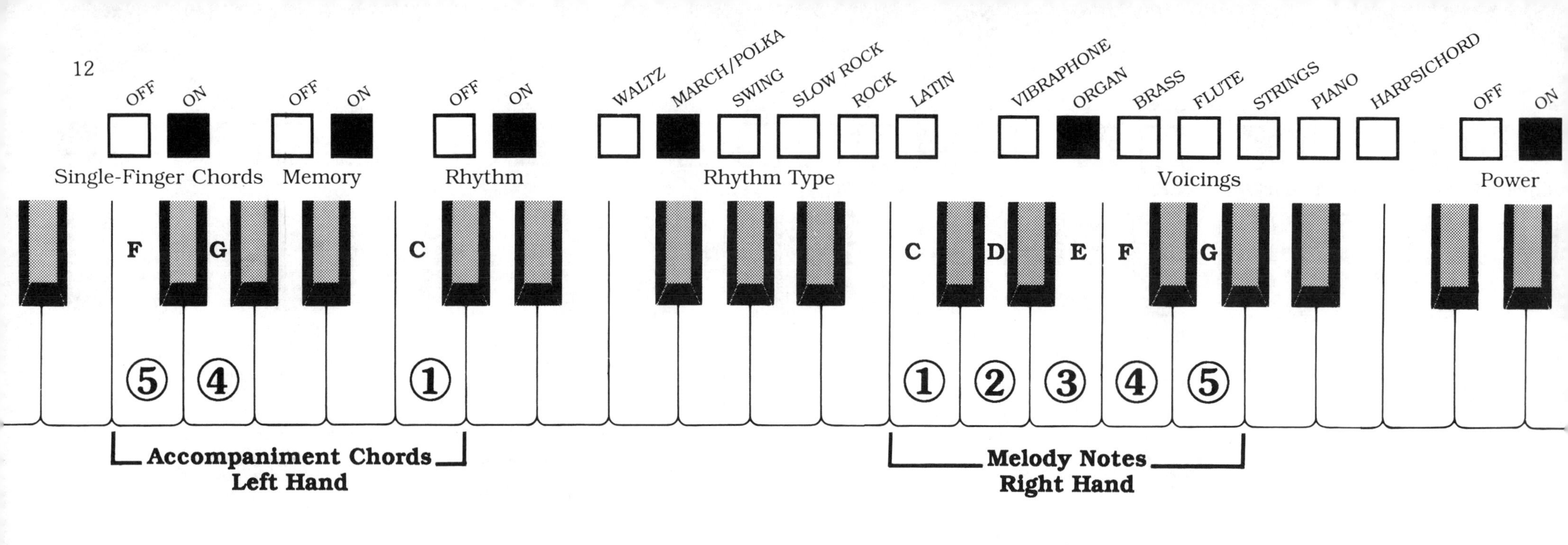

Keyboard Song in Quarter Notes

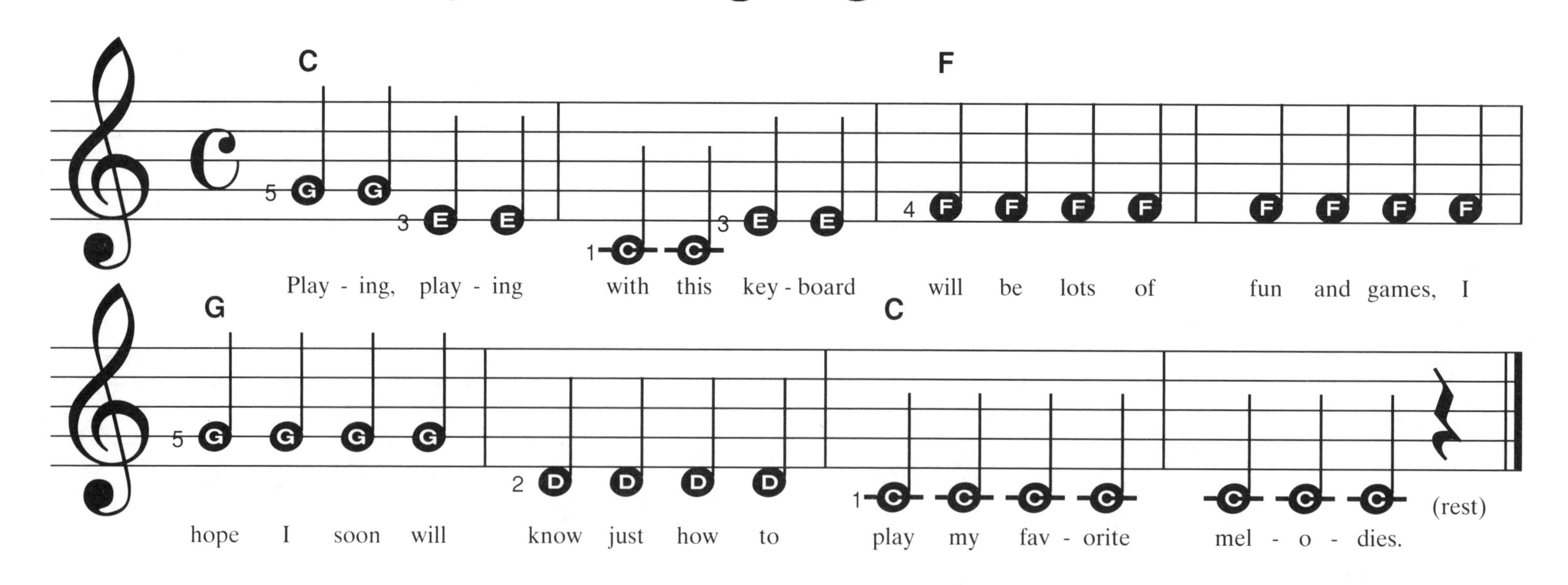

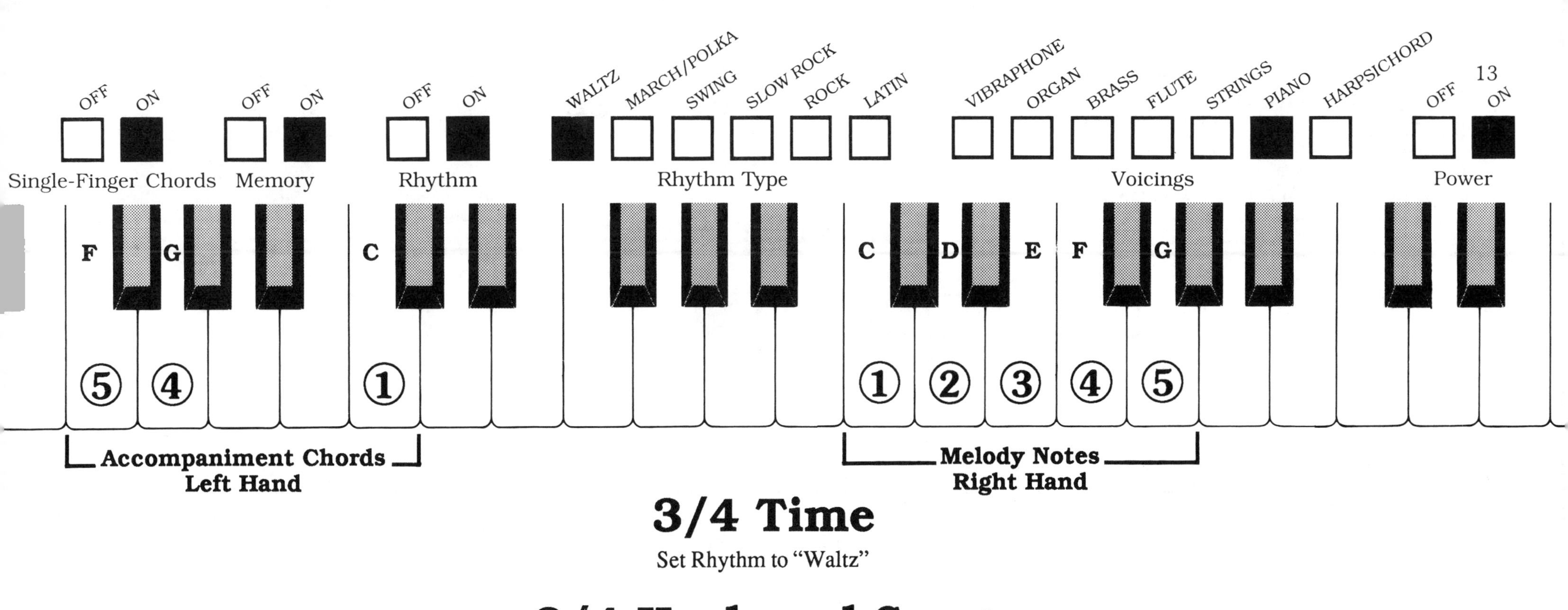

3/4 Time

Set Rhythm to "Waltz"

3/4 Keyboard Song

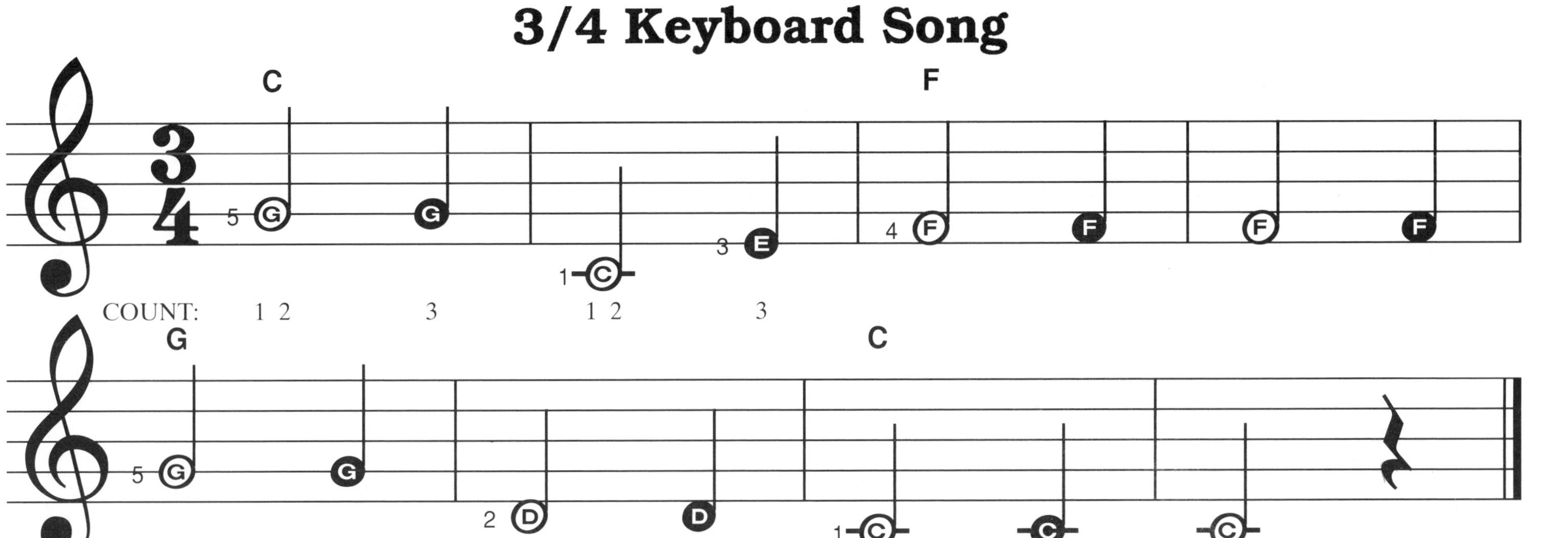

1st	**Practice right hand.**
2nd	**Practice left hand.**
3rd	**Practice both hands together.**

Dotted Half Note

This note receives 3 counts.

German Waltz

OFF / ON	OFF / ON	OFF / ON	WALTZ	OBOE or FLUTE
Single-Finger Chords	Memory	Rhythm	Rhythm Type	Voicings

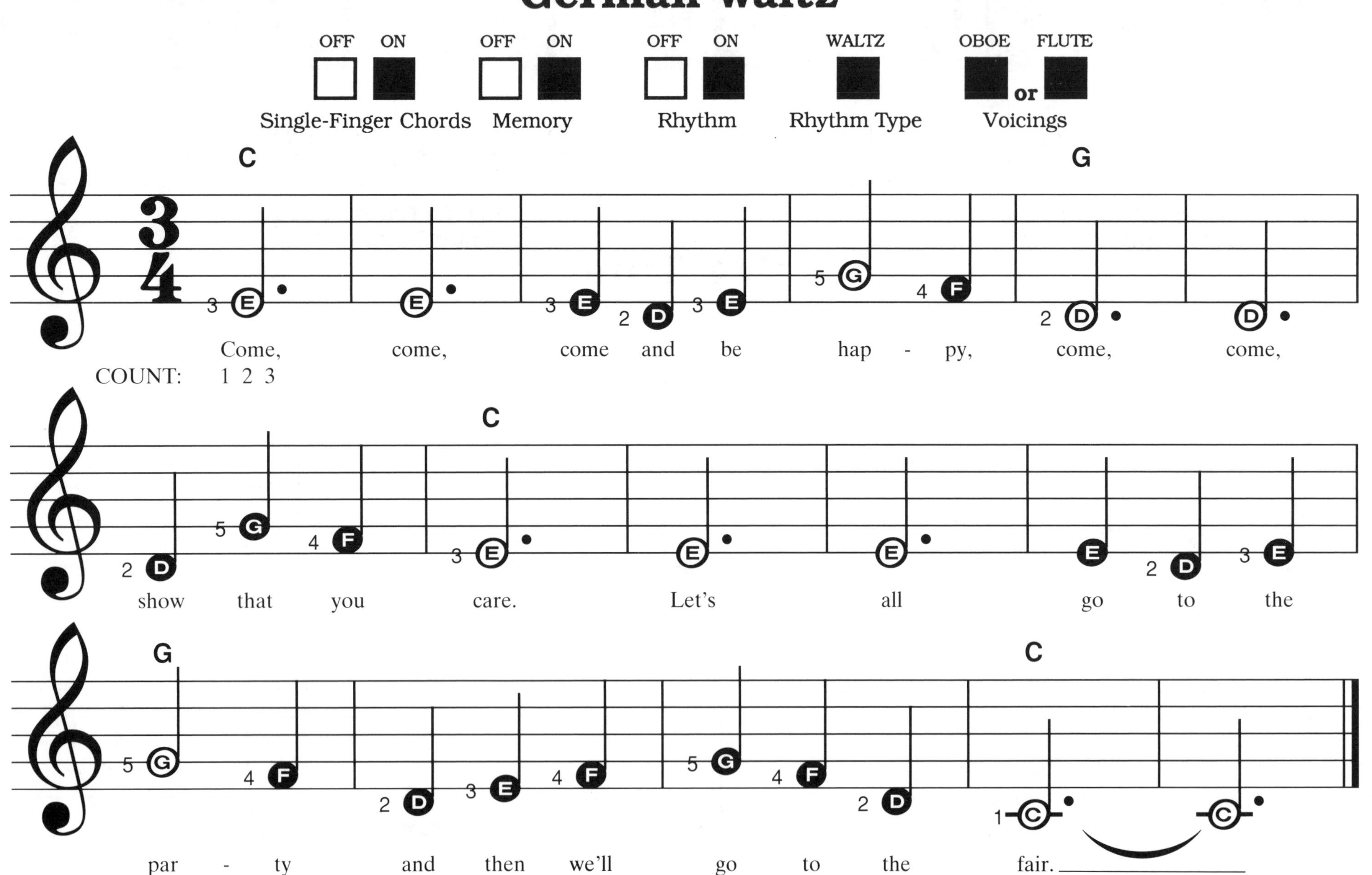

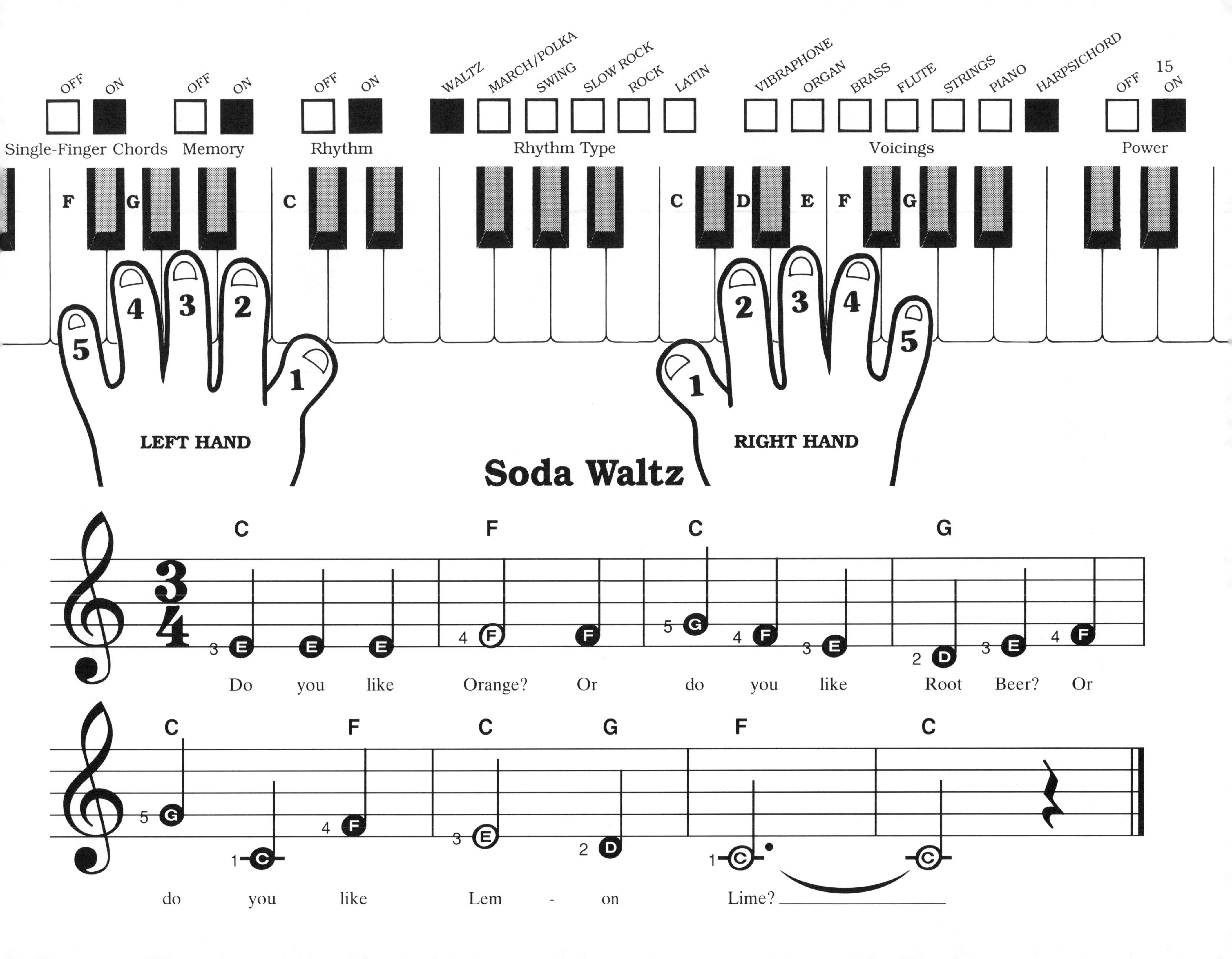
OFF
ON
OFF
ON
OFF
ON
WALTZ
MARCH/POLKA
SWING
SLOW ROCK
ROCK
LATIN
VIBRAPHONE
ORGAN
BRASS
FLUTE
STRINGS
PIANO
HARPSICHORD
OFF
15
ON
Single-Finger Chords
Memory
Rhythm
Rhythm Type
Voicings
Power
F
G
C
C
D
E
F
G
5
4
3
2
1
2
3
4
5
1
LEFT HAND
RIGHT HAND
Soda Waltz
C
F
C
G
Do you like Orange? Or do you like Root Beer? Or
C
F
C
G
F
C
do you like Lem - on Lime?

When this sign appears, play only the first note. Hold the second note.

The Tie

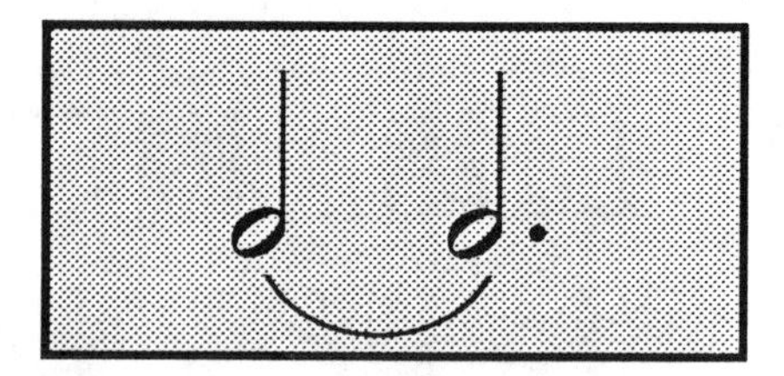

Beautiful Blue Eyes

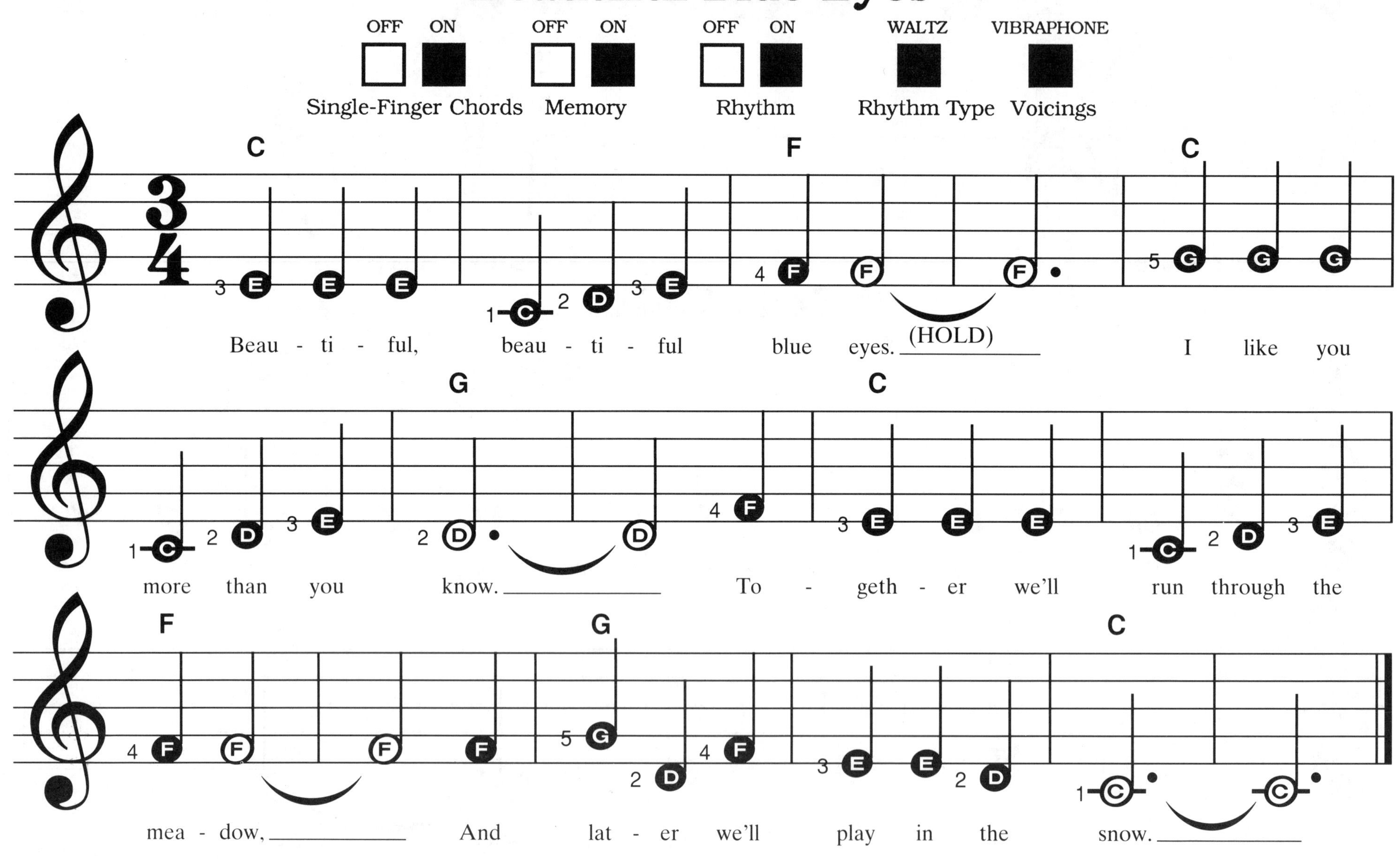

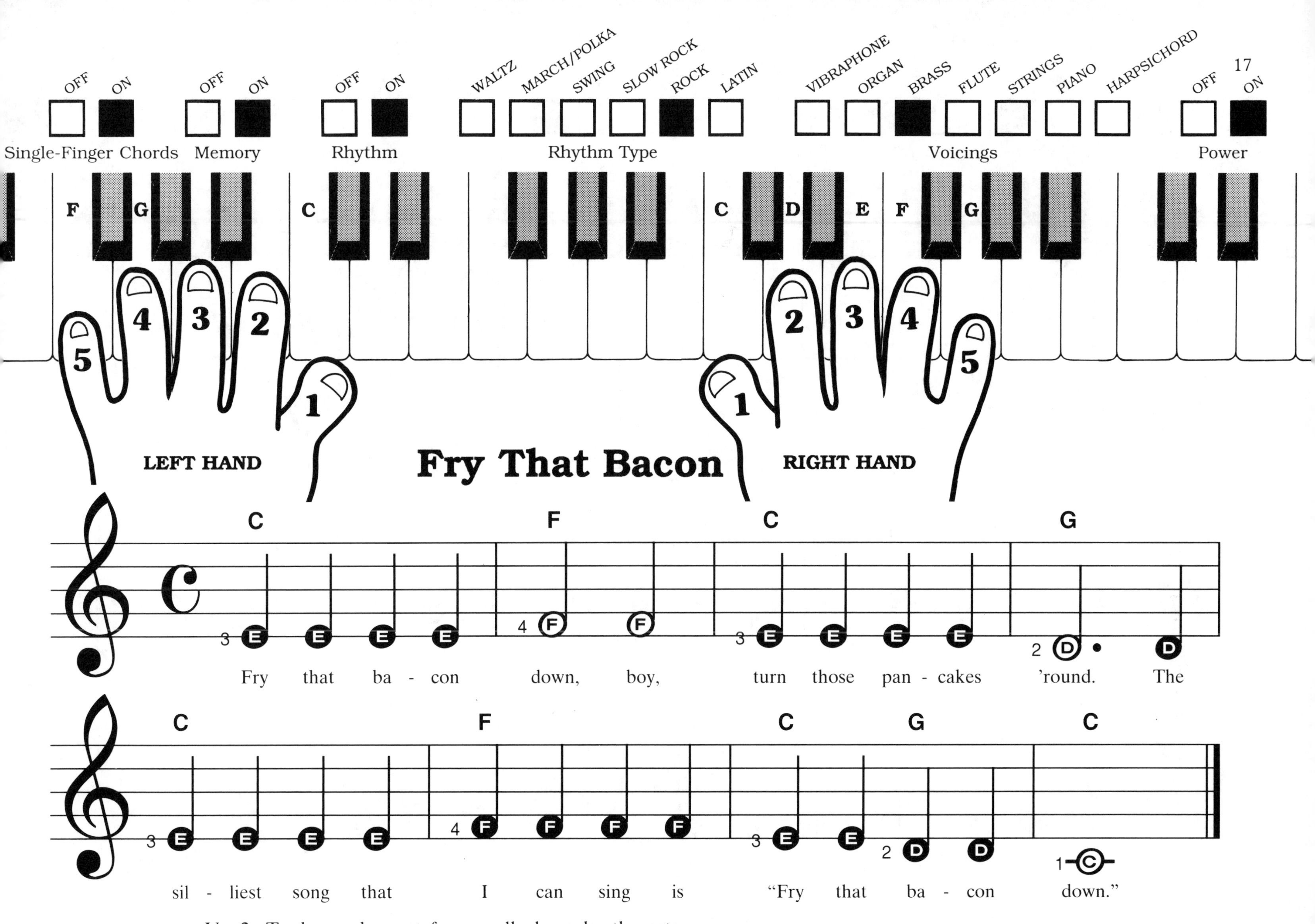

Vs. 2 Took my dog out for a walk down by the gate,
He nipped a jogger and a biker, sure thought he was great! [Make up your own verses]

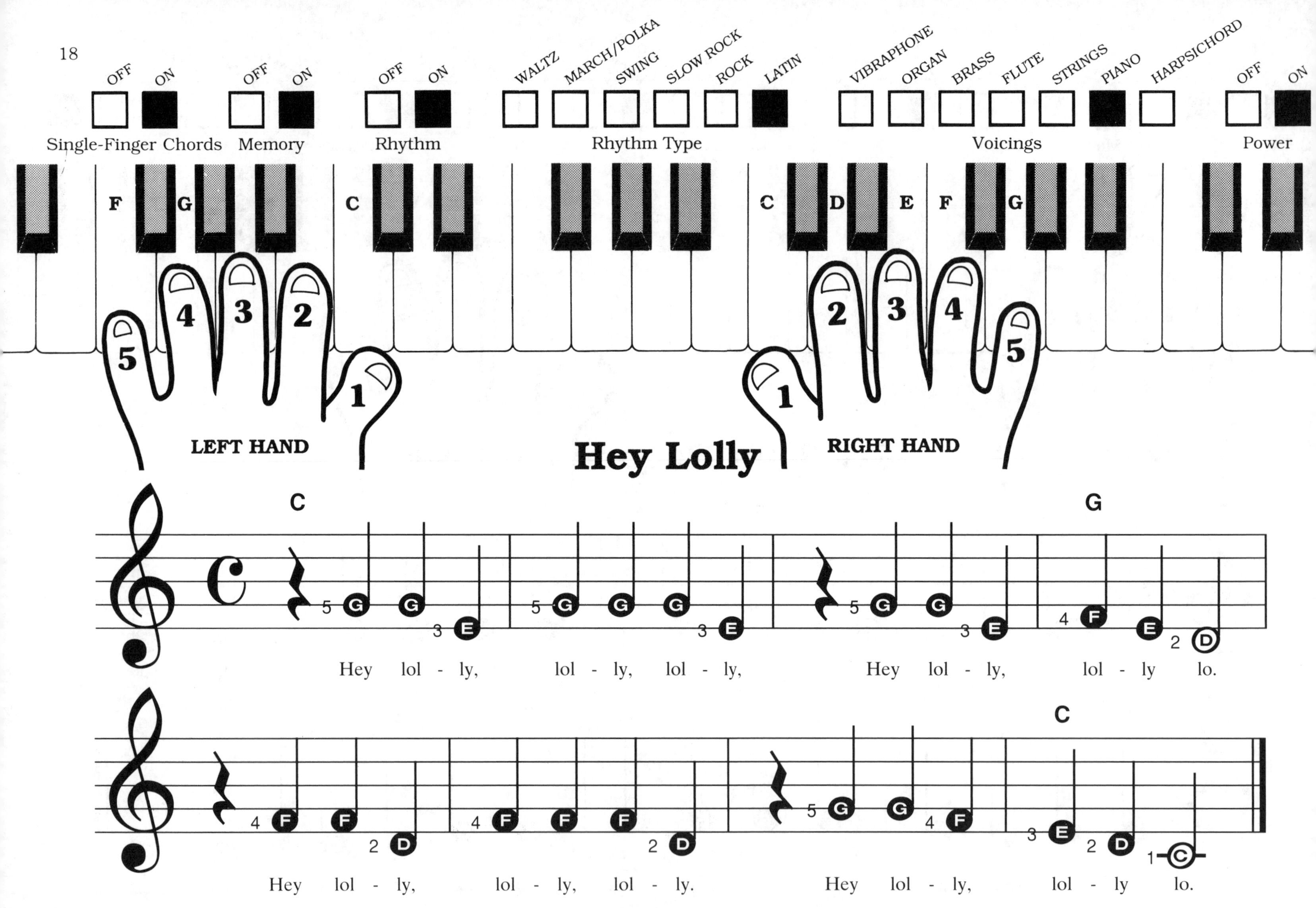

Vs. 2. Seems like I'm making music, Now I've begun to play,
This keyboard sure is easy, I think I'll play all day.

Eighth Notes

Eighth notes look like this  or this 

2 eighth notes  = 1 quarter note 

Say & Play

Say the words to the following songs while you play them on your keyboard.

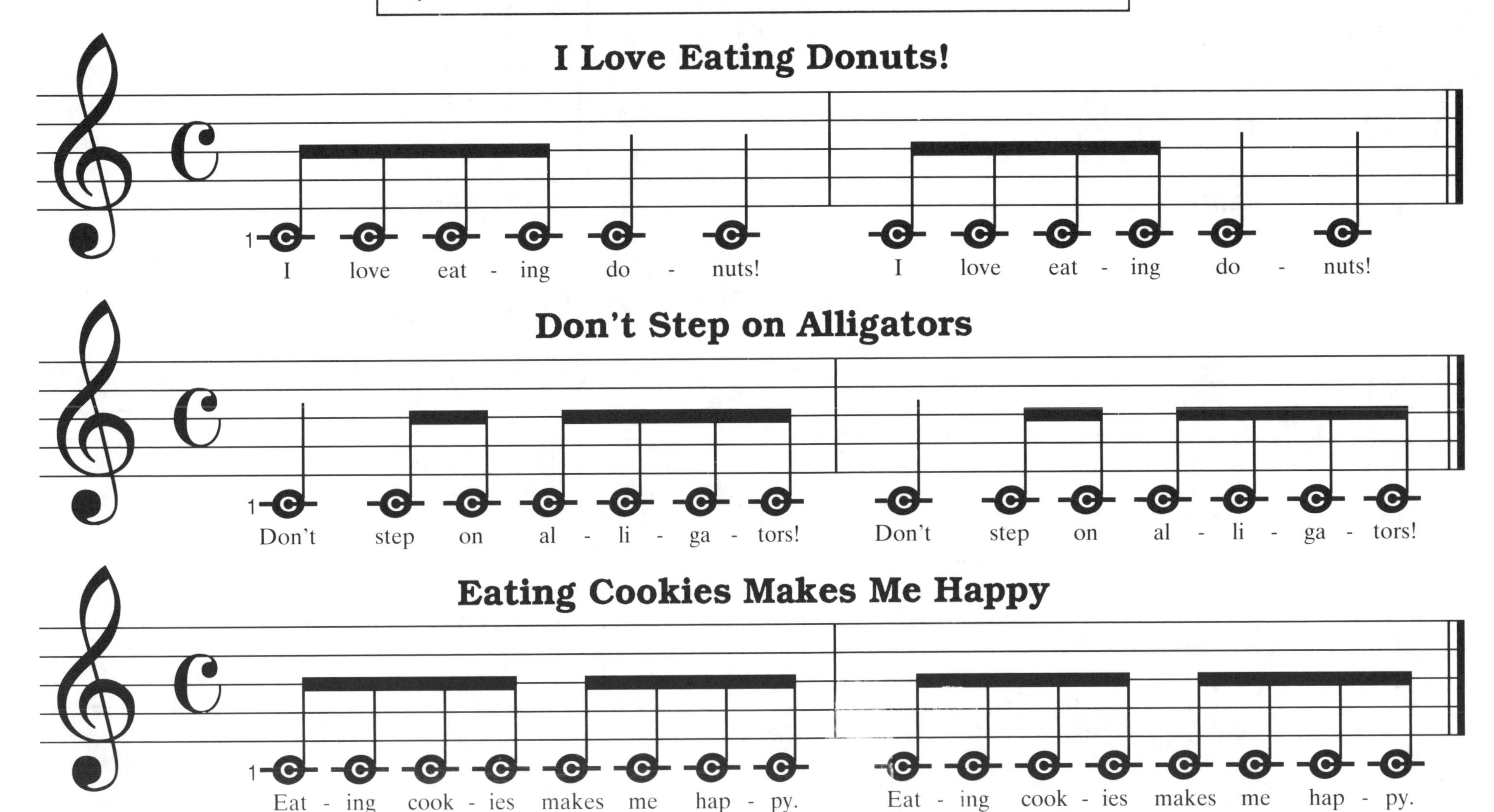

OFF
ON
Single-Finger Chords
OFF
ON
Memory
OFF
ON
Rhythm
WALTZ
MARCH/POLKA
SWING
SLOW ROCK
ROCK
LATIN
Rhythm Type
VIBRAPHONE
ORGAN
BRASS
FLUTE
STRINGS
PIANO
HARPSICHORD
Voicings
OFF
ON
Power
F
G
C
C
D
E
F
G
LEFT HAND
RIGHT HAND
Once There Were Three Fishermen
C
G
C
Once there were three fish - er - men.
G
C
Once there were three fish - er - men.
Fish - er, fish - er, men, men, men.

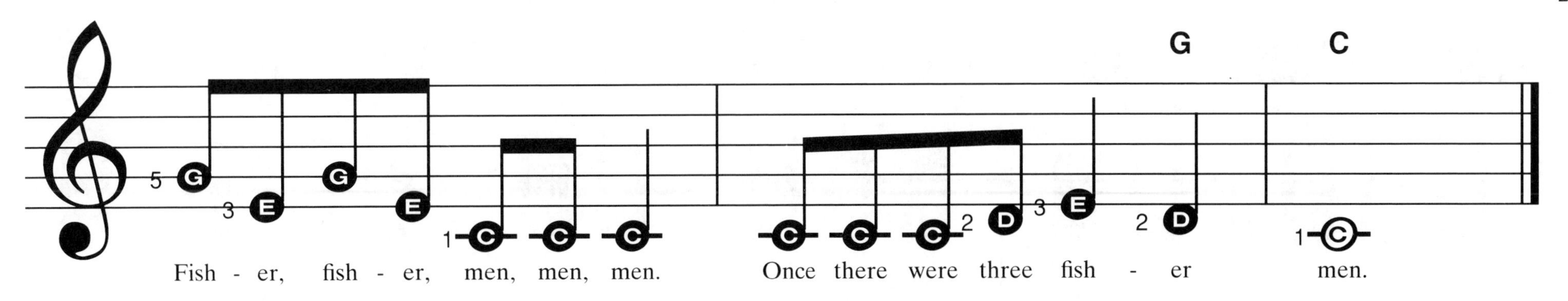

Vs. 2. First one's name was Abraham
(Repeat)
Abra, Abra, ham, ham, ham
(Repeat)
First one's name was Abraham

Vs. 3. Second's name was Isaac.
Isy, Isy, ac, ac, ac.

Vs. 4. Third one's name was Jacob
Jakey, Jakey, cub, cub, cub.

Vs. 5. Wish they'd gone to Amsterdam.
Amster, Amster, dam, dam, dam.

Lightly Row

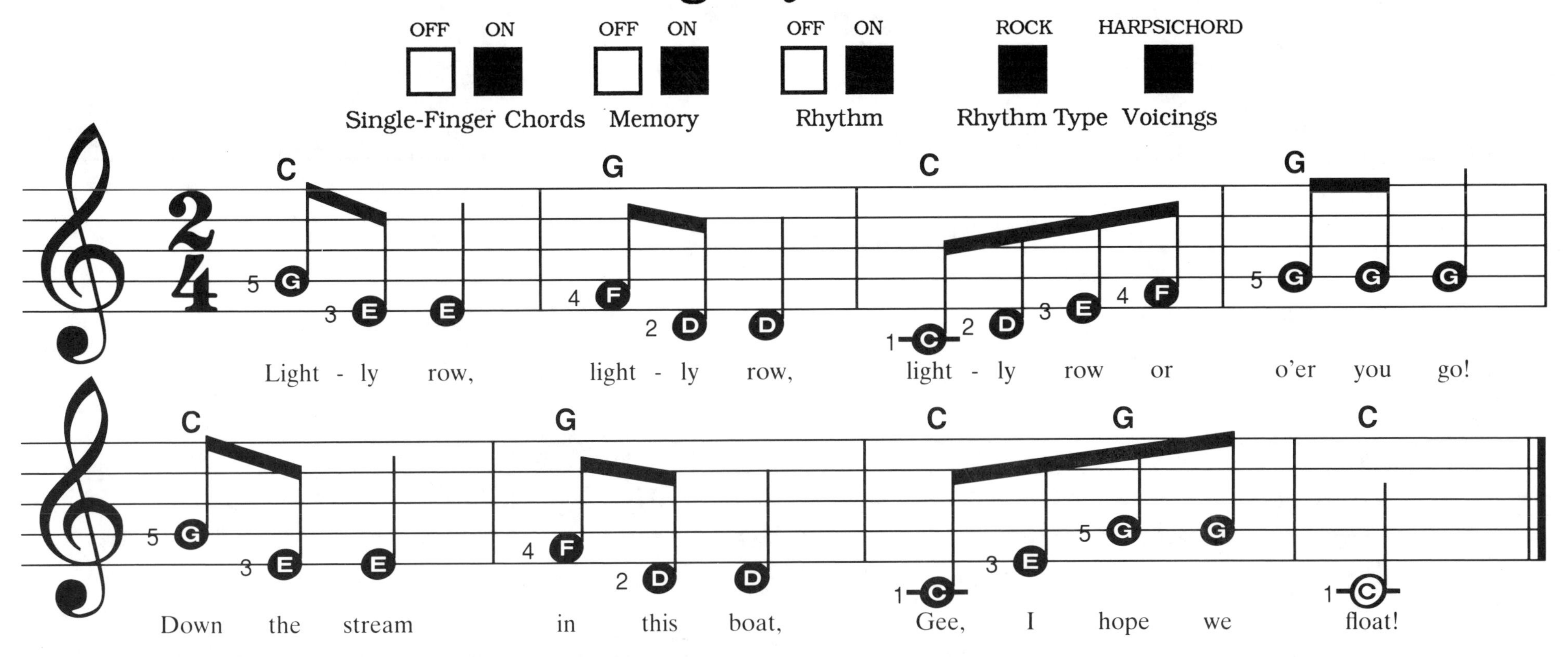

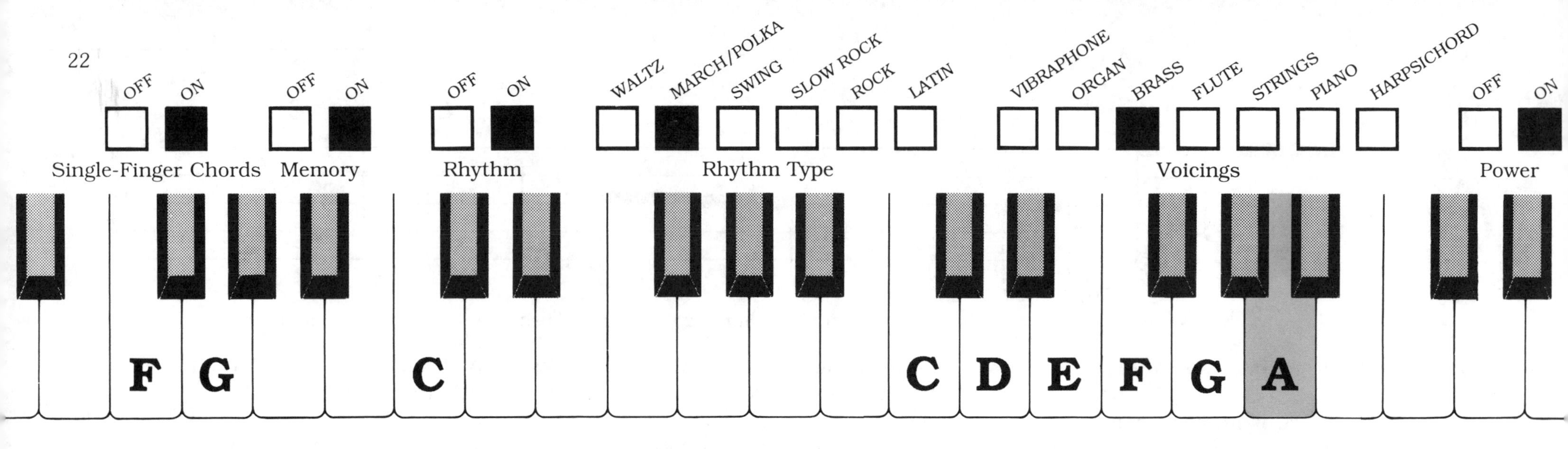

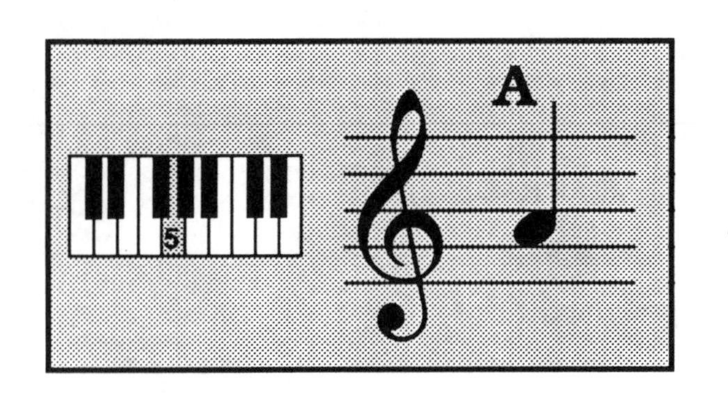

A New Note "A"

To play "A," you will need to move your hand to the right. A is played with the little finger of the right hand. In the following piece, look carefully at the right-hand finger numbers by each note.

This Old Man

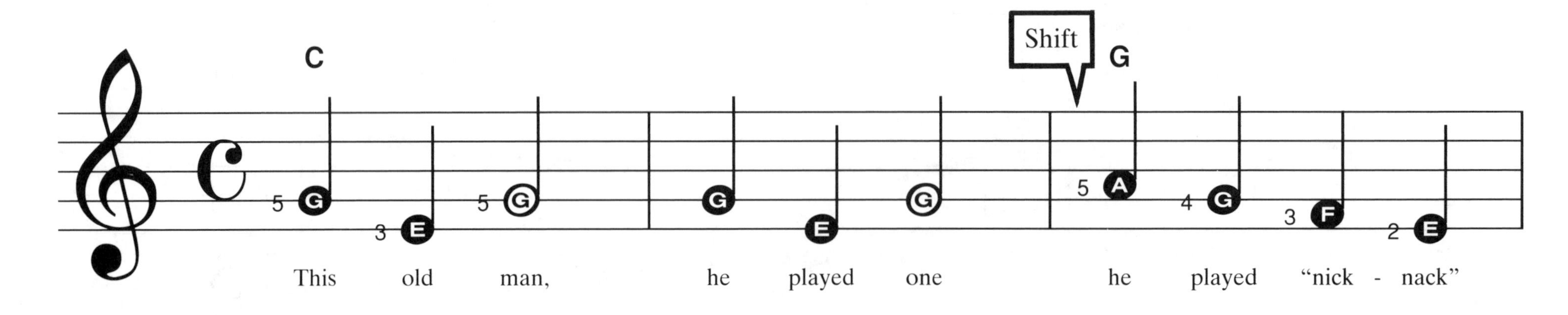

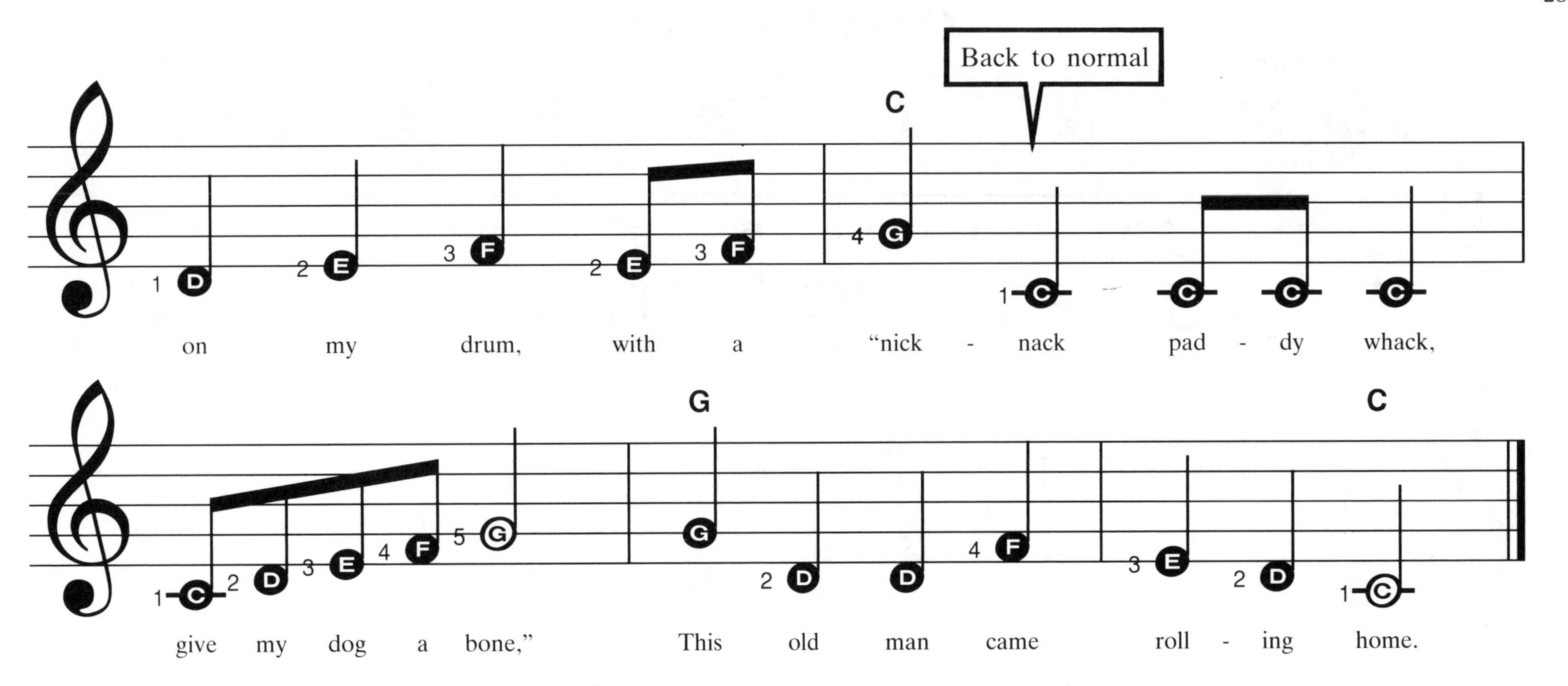

On the following song you will shift your right hand while playing. Study the two playing positions!

Crawdad Song

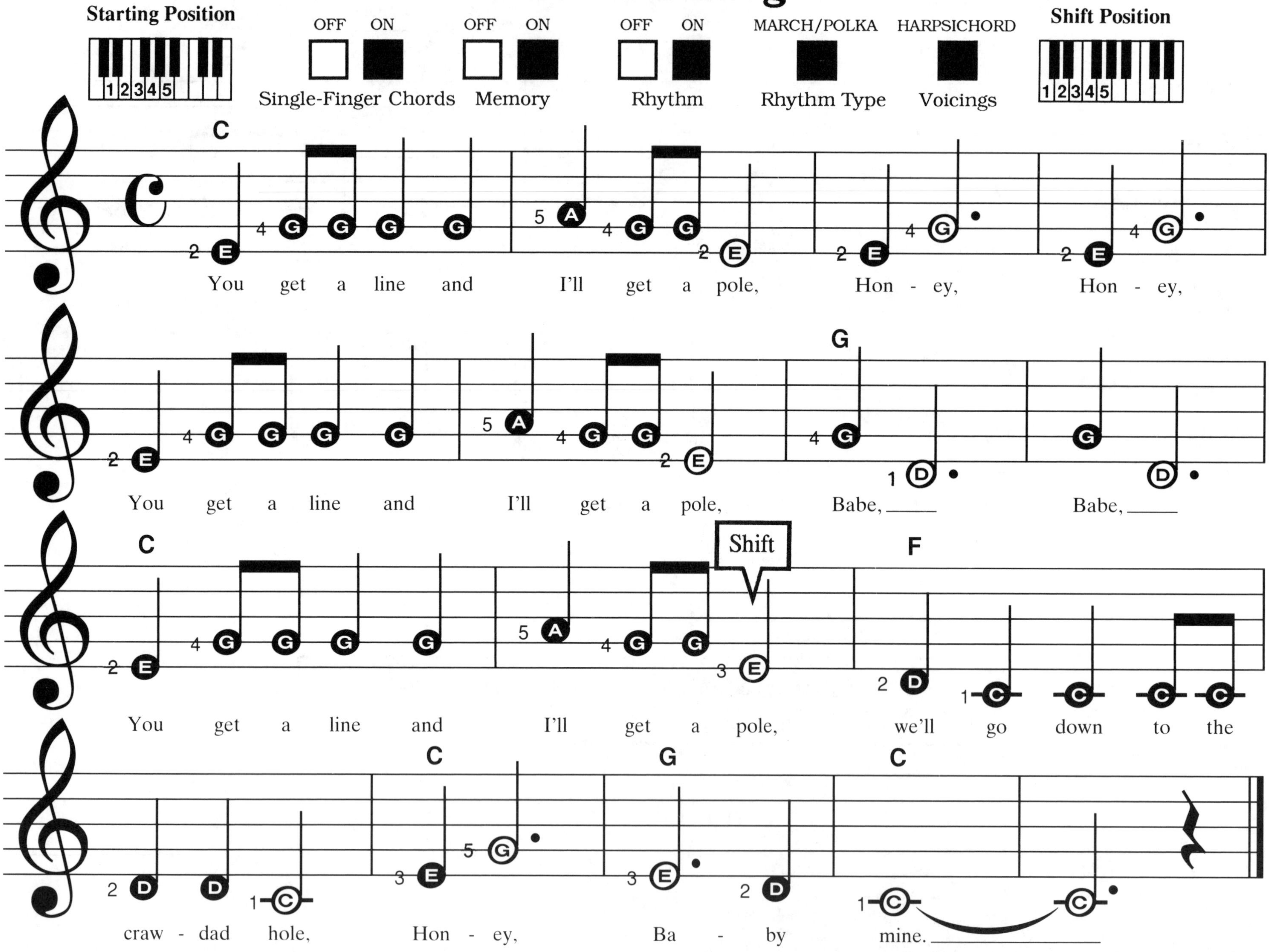

Starting Position 1 2 3 4 5

Single-Finger Chords: OFF ON
Memory: OFF ON
Rhythm: OFF ON
Rhythm Type: MARCH/POLKA
Voicings: HARPSICHORD

Shift Position 1 2 3 4 5

C
You get a line and I'll get a pole, Hon - ey, Hon - ey,

G
You get a line and I'll get a pole, Babe, ___ Babe, ___

C F
You get a line and I'll get a pole, (Shift) we'll go down to the

C G C
craw - dad hole, Hon - ey, Ba - by mine. ___

Pick-Up Notes

Some songs begin with a few preparatory or lead-in notes. These are called "pick-up notes." Do not play a left-hand chord on these notes. Play your chord on the first beat of the first full measure of the song. Follow the finger numbers as shown. Watch for shifts!

Oh! Susanna

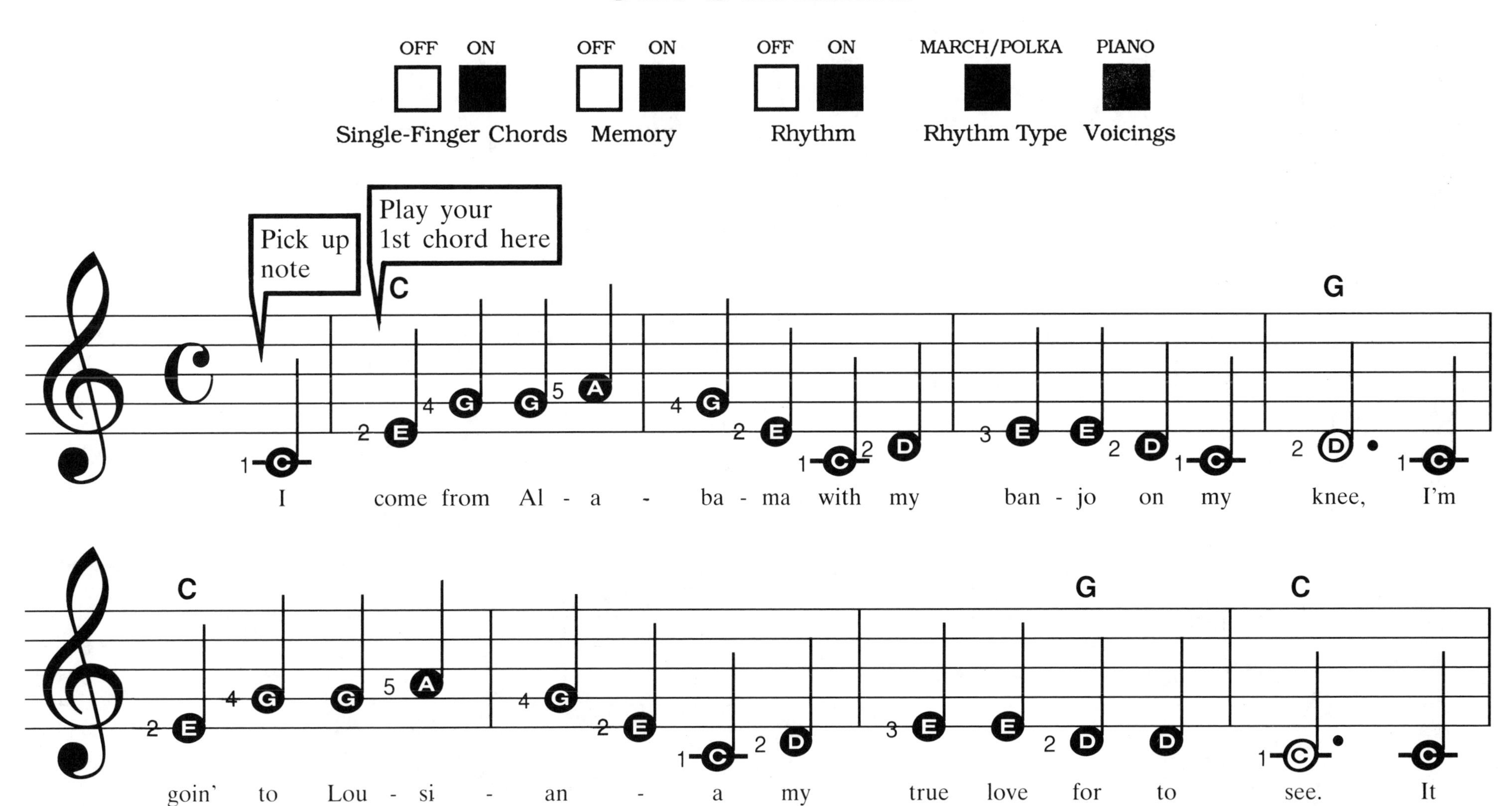

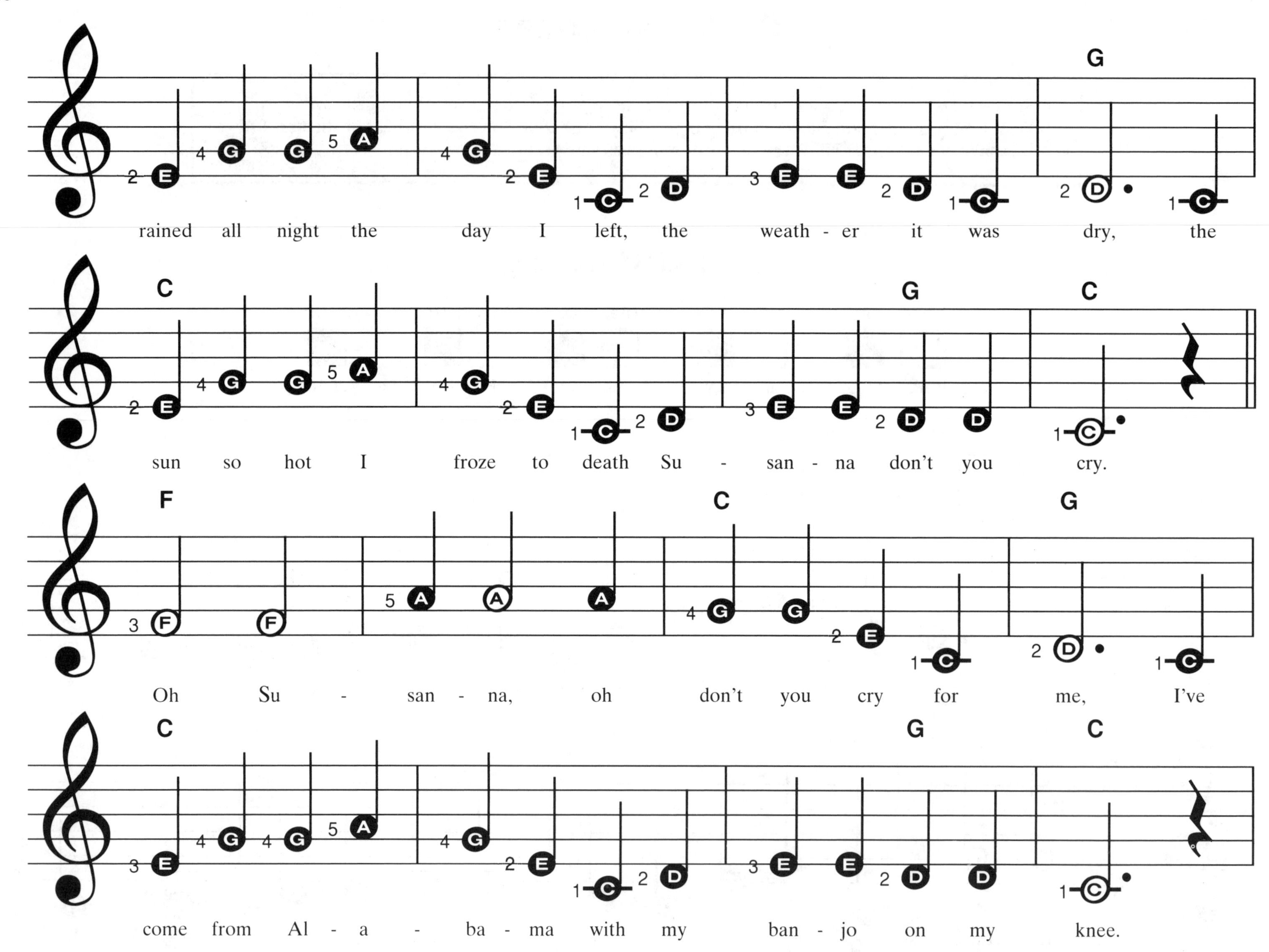
G
rained all night the day I left, the weath - er it was dry, the
C G C
sun so hot I froze to death Su - san - na don't you cry.
F C G
Oh Su - san - na, oh don't you cry for me, I've
C G C
come from Al - a - ba - ma with my ban - jo on my knee.

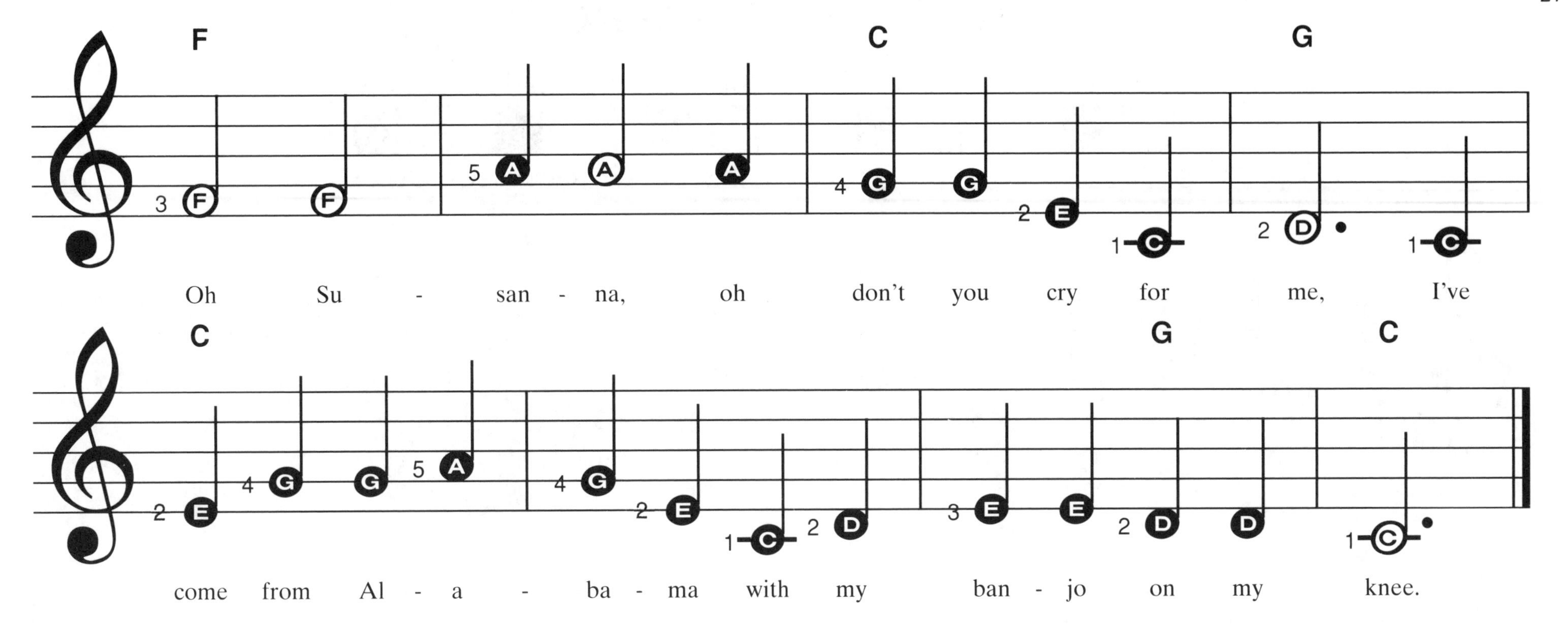

Repeat Sign

A repeat sign :‖ means to go back to the beginning or to a sign that looks like this ‖:
The first time through the song, you take the first ending. The second time through, you take the second ending.

A-Tisket, A-Tasket

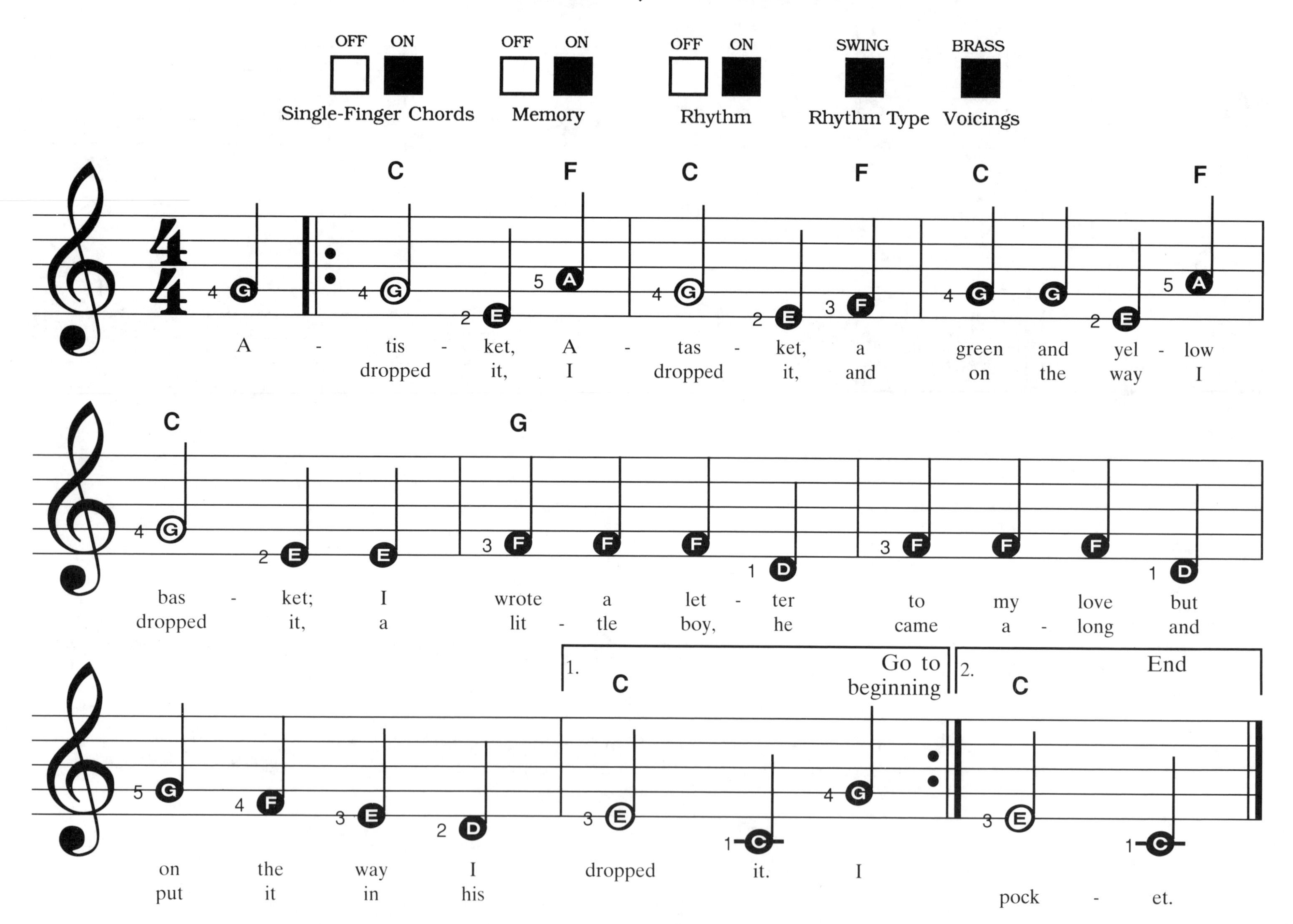

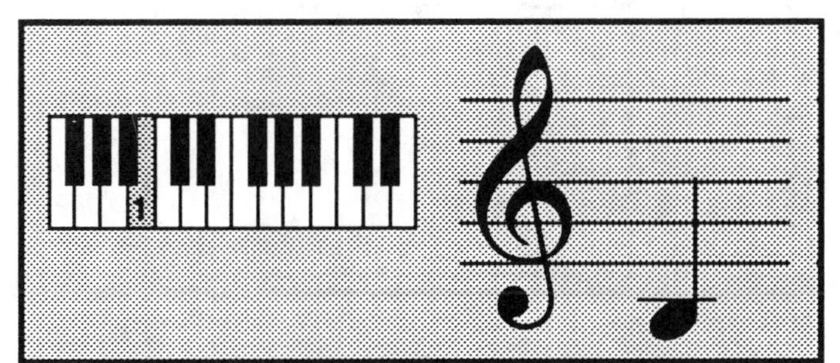

Low B

To play low B, you will need to move your hand to the left. Low B is played with the thumb of the right hand.

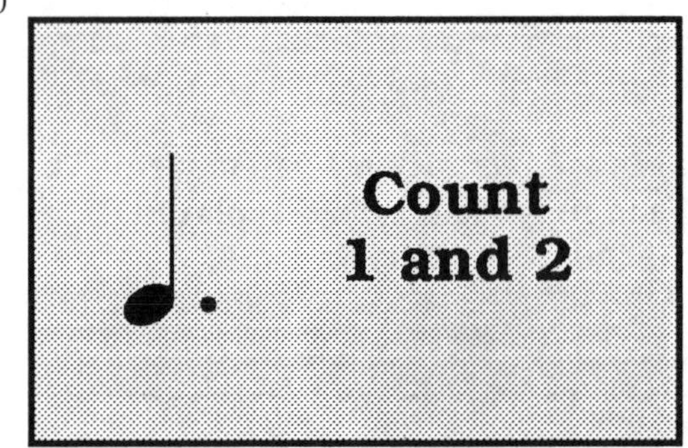

Dotted Quarter Note

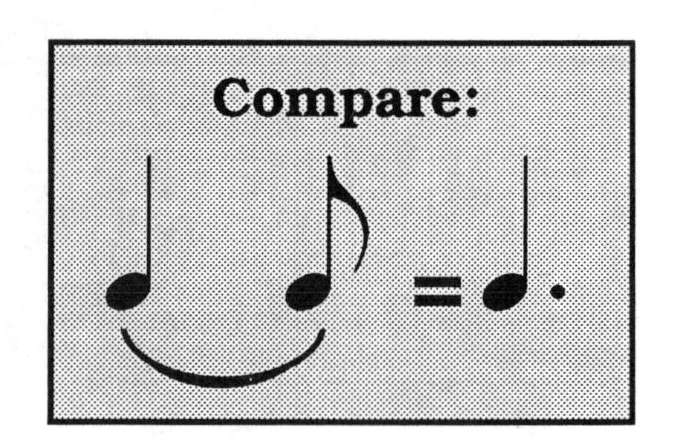

Study #1

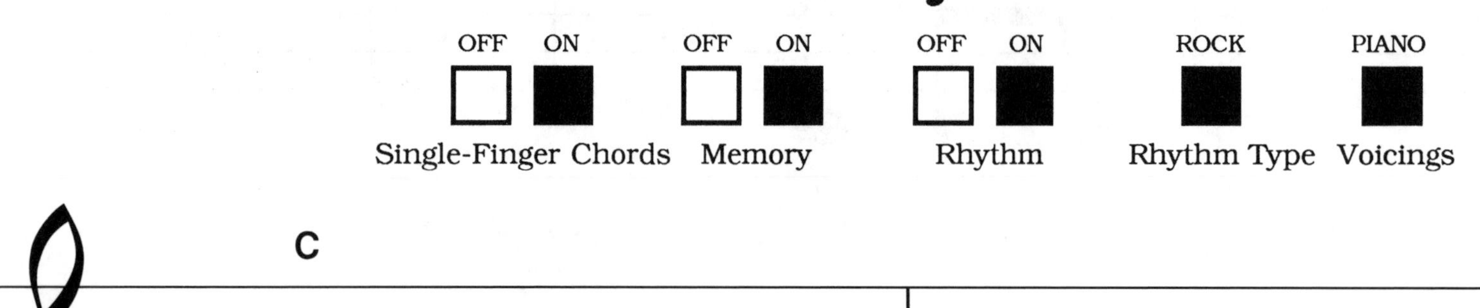

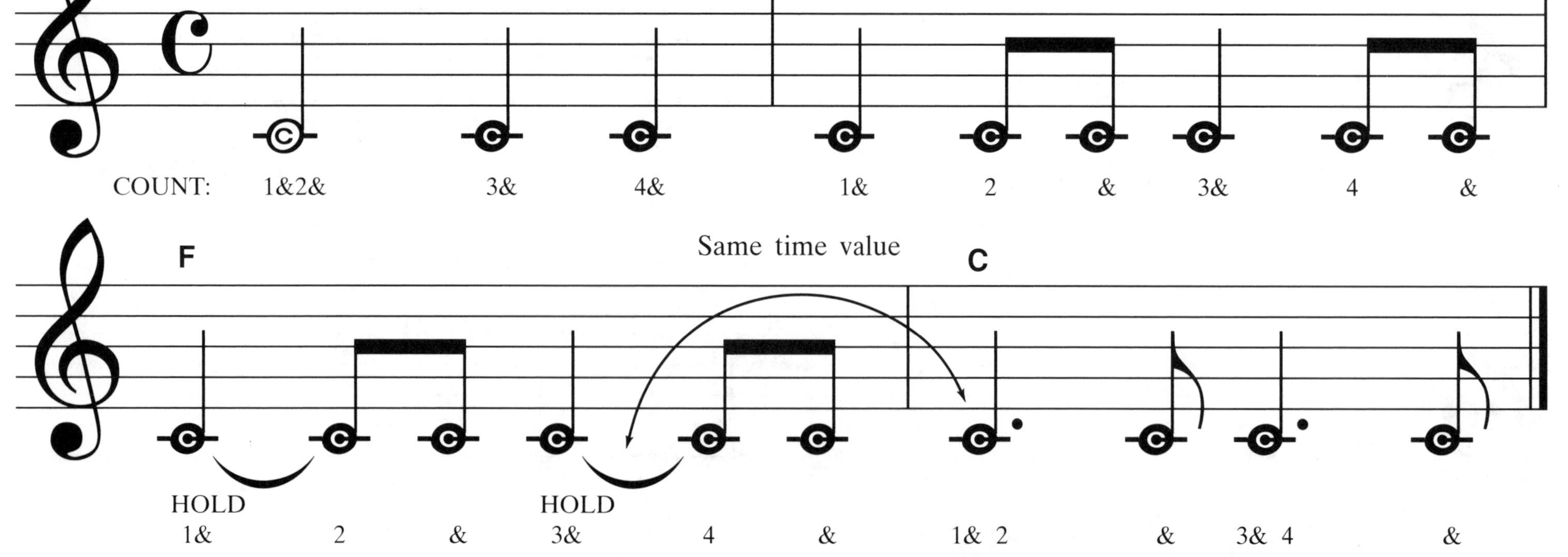

OFF ON
Single-Finger Chords
OFF ON
Memory
Kum Ba Ya
OFF ON
Rhythm
LATIN
Rhythm Type
FLUTE
Voicings
C F C
Some - one's sing - ing, Lord. Kum - ba - ya.
F G
Some - one's sing - ing, Lord. Kum - ba - ya.
C F C
Some - one's sing - ing, Lord. Kum - ba - ya.
F C G C
Oh, Lord. Kum - ba - ya.
Vs. 2. Someone's crying, Lord. Kum-ba-ya.
Vs. 3. Someone's praying, Lord. Kum-ba-ya.

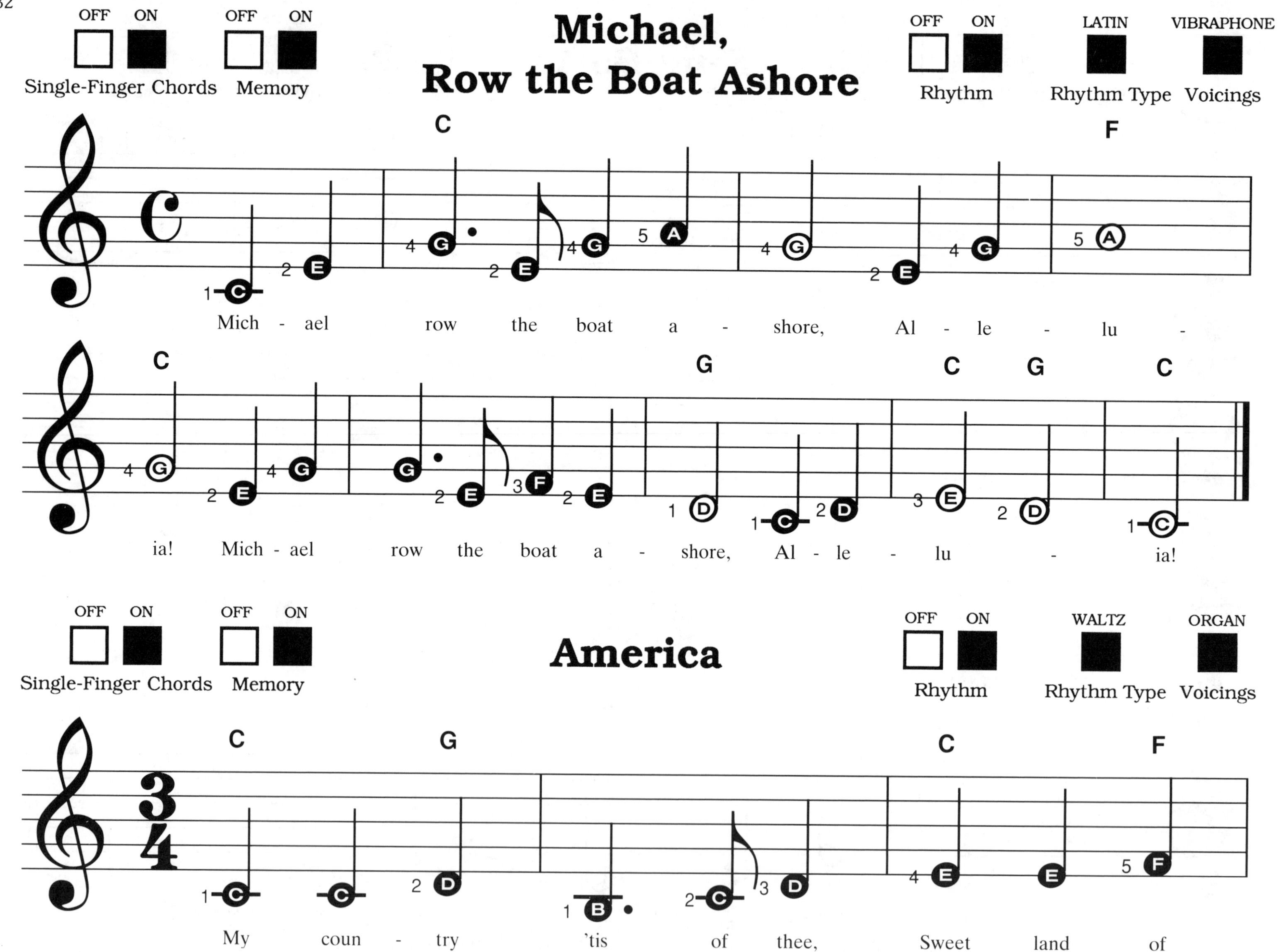
OFF ON
Single-Finger Chords
OFF ON
Memory
Michael,
Row the Boat Ashore
OFF ON
Rhythm
LATIN
Rhythm Type
VIBRAPHONE
Voicings
C F
Mich - ael row the boat a - shore, Al - le - lu -
C G C G C
ia! Mich - ael row the boat a - shore, Al - le - lu - ia!
OFF ON
Single-Finger Chords
OFF ON
Memory
America
OFF ON
Rhythm
WALTZ
Rhythm Type
ORGAN
Voicings
C G C F
My coun - try 'tis of thee, Sweet land of

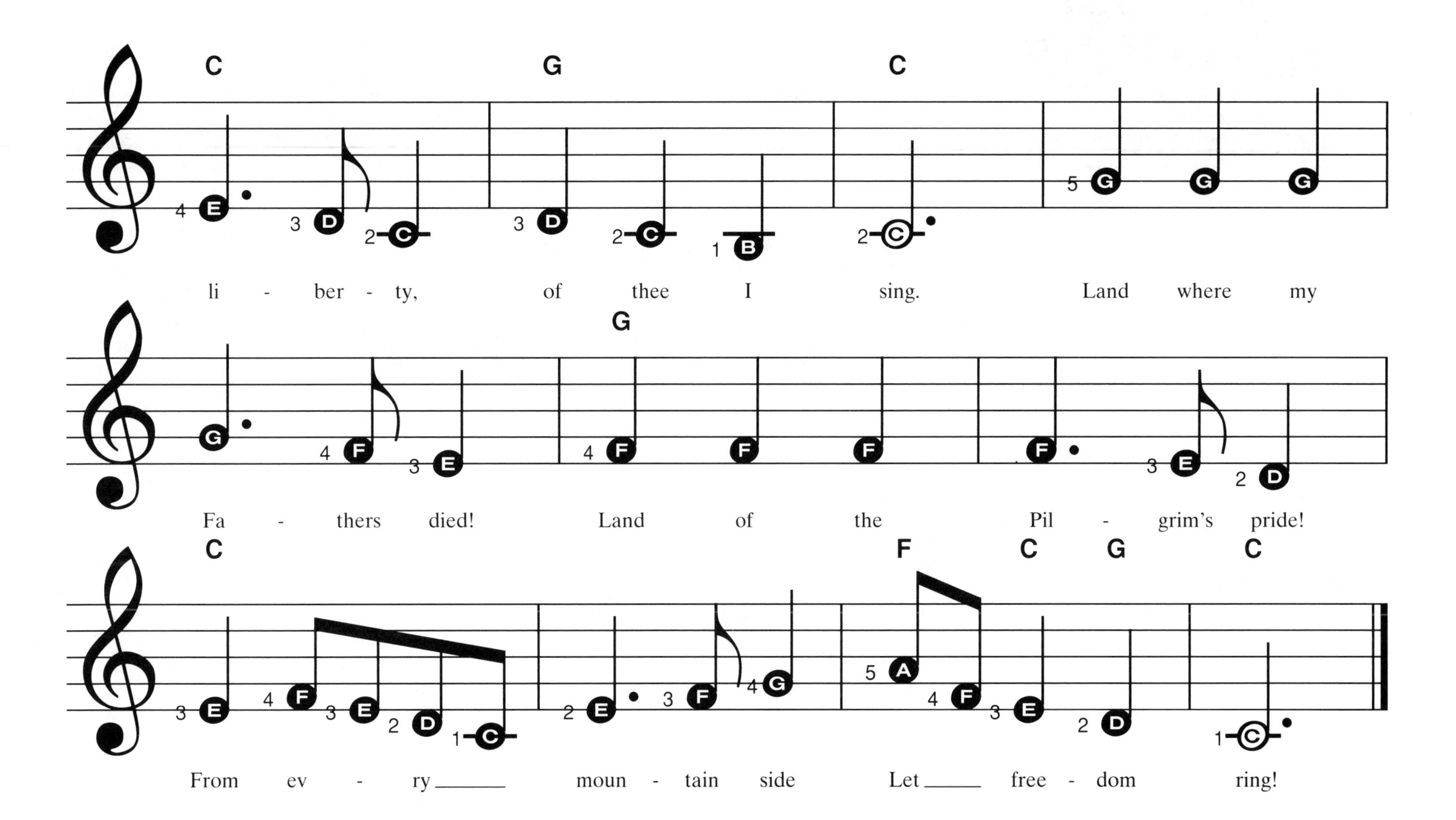
C G C
li - ber - ty, of thee I sing. Land where my
G
Fa - thers died! Land of the Pil - grim's pride!
C F C G C
From ev - ry mountain side Let freedom ring!

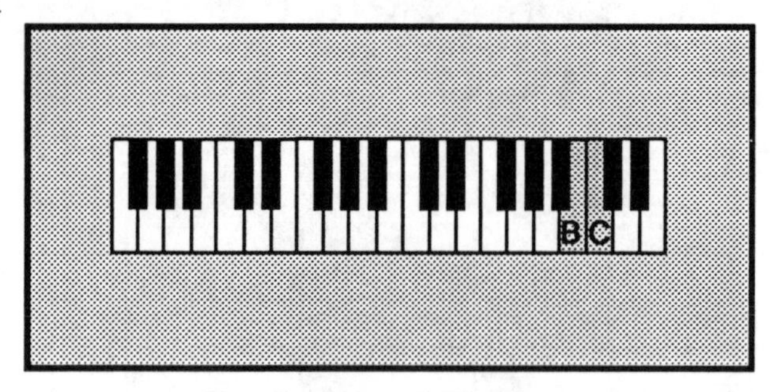

High B and C

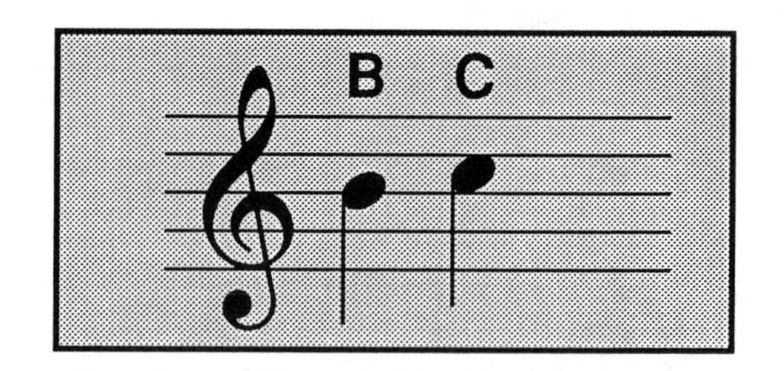

Camptown Races

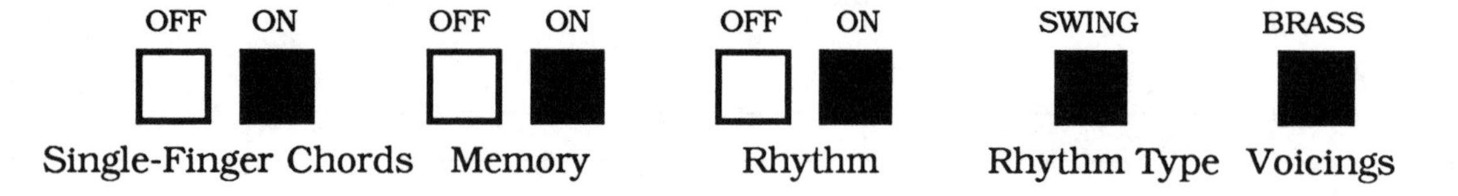

[Watch the finger numbers. You will need to shift your right hand position during this piece.]

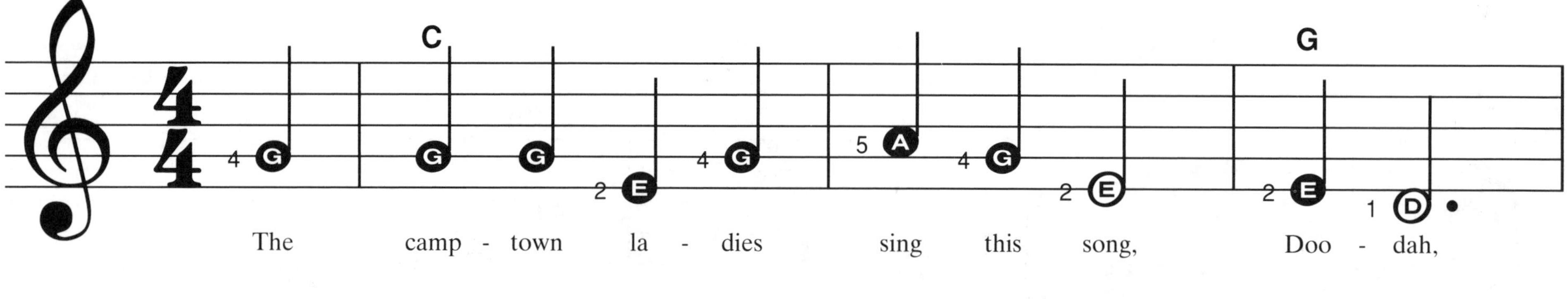

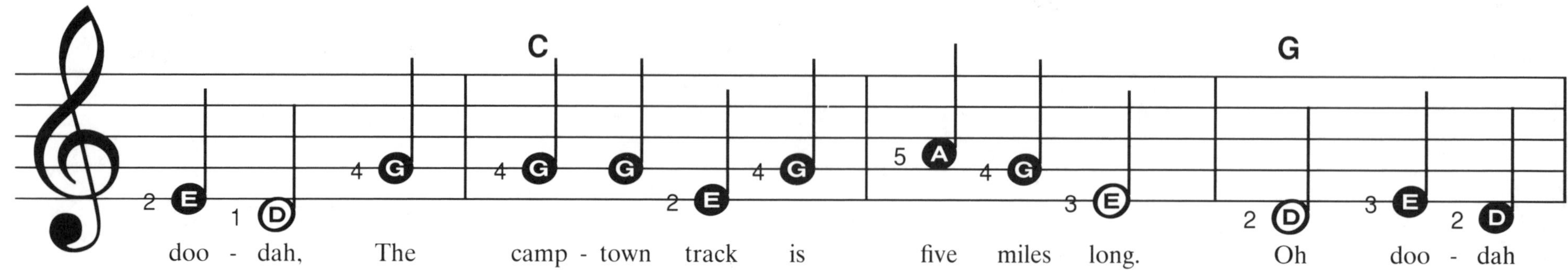

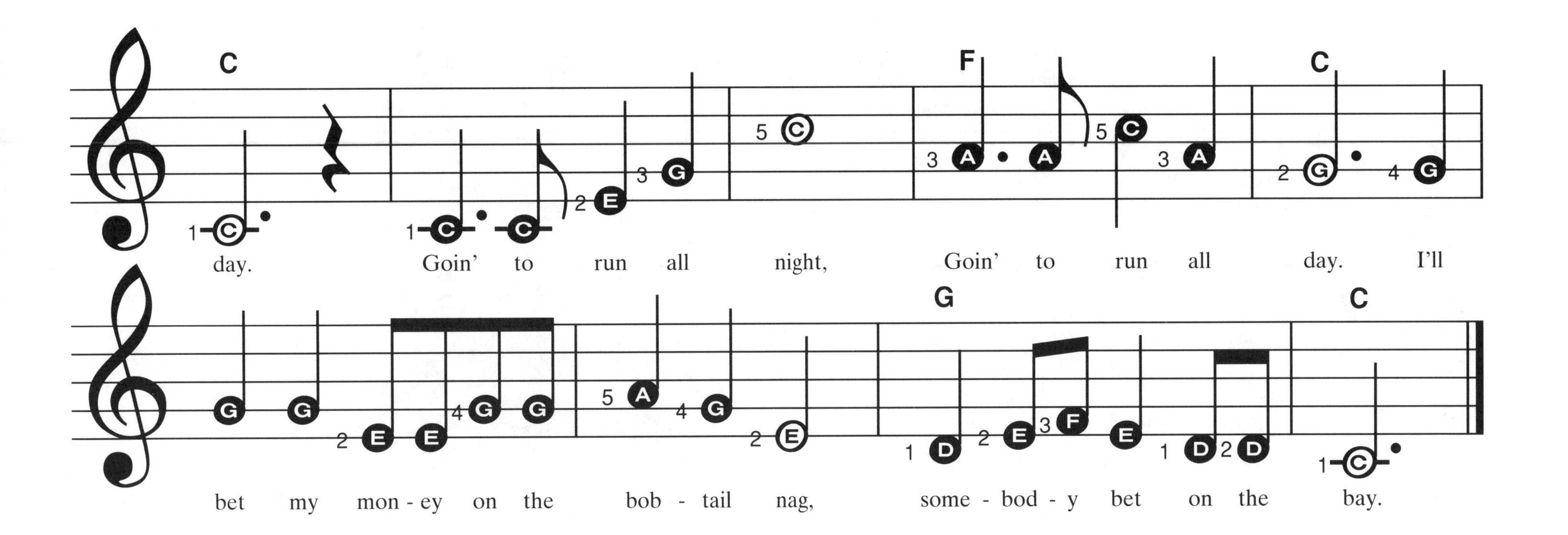
C
F
C
day. Goin' to run all night, Goin' to run all day. I'll
G
C
bet my mon - ey on the bob - tail nag, some - bod - y bet on the bay.

Kookaburra

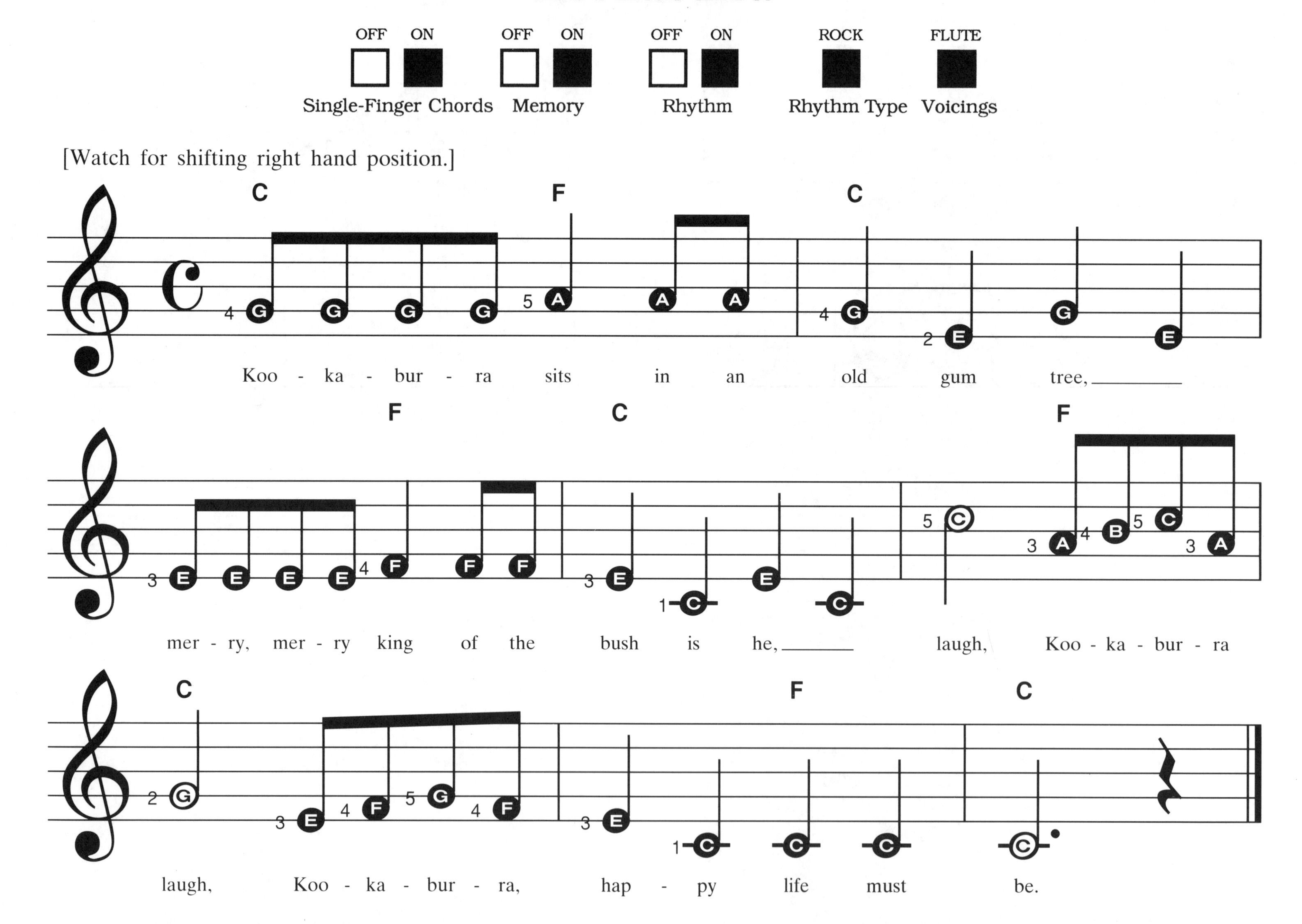
OFF ON
Single-Finger Chords
OFF ON
Memory
OFF ON
Rhythm
ROCK
Rhythm Type
FLUTE
Voicings
[Watch for shifting right hand position.]
C F C
Koo - ka - bur - ra sits in an old gum tree,
F C F
mer - ry, mer - ry king of the bush is he,
laugh, Koo - ka - bur - ra
C F C
laugh, Koo - ka - bur - ra, hap - py life must be.

G7 Chord

A dominant 7th chord is important to know. A chord with a "7" by it is a dominant 7th chord. (Thus we have "G7" or "G dominant 7.") A 7th chord usually goes back to the original chord in a key. Thus G7 leads us back to C. There are two ways of playing a G7 chord in "Single-Finger Chords" mode. If you have a Casio, Bontempi, or most other keyboards (except Yamaha), play your G7 chord as shown below. (Play the note of the chord name —G— and the next two white keys above it.)

G7 on Casio, Bontempi, Etc.

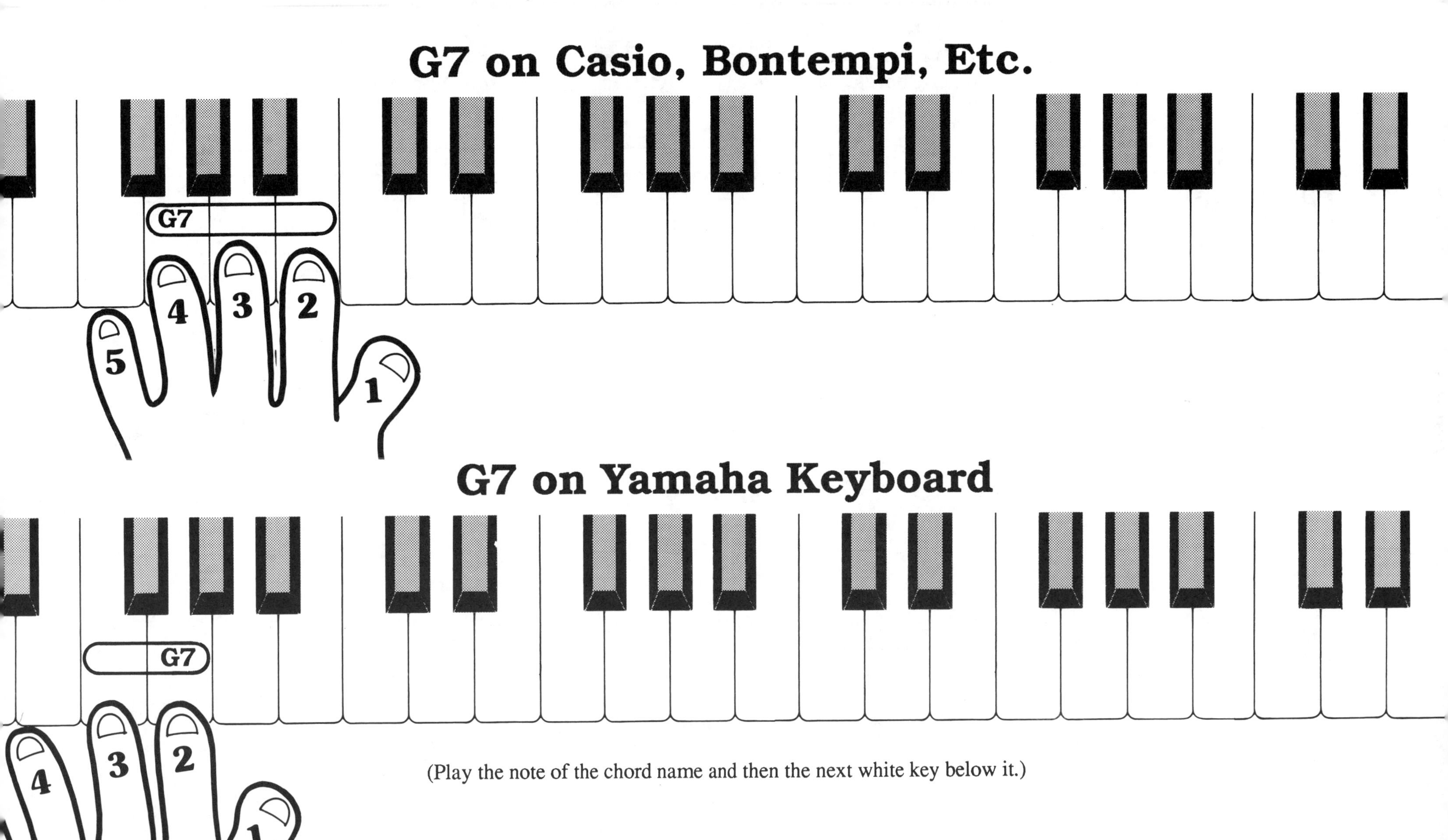

G7 on Yamaha Keyboard

(Play the note of the chord name and then the next white key below it.)

Songs Using G7

(Be sure to practice the chord accompaniment before adding the right-hand melody.)

Oh, Dear, What Can the Matter Be?

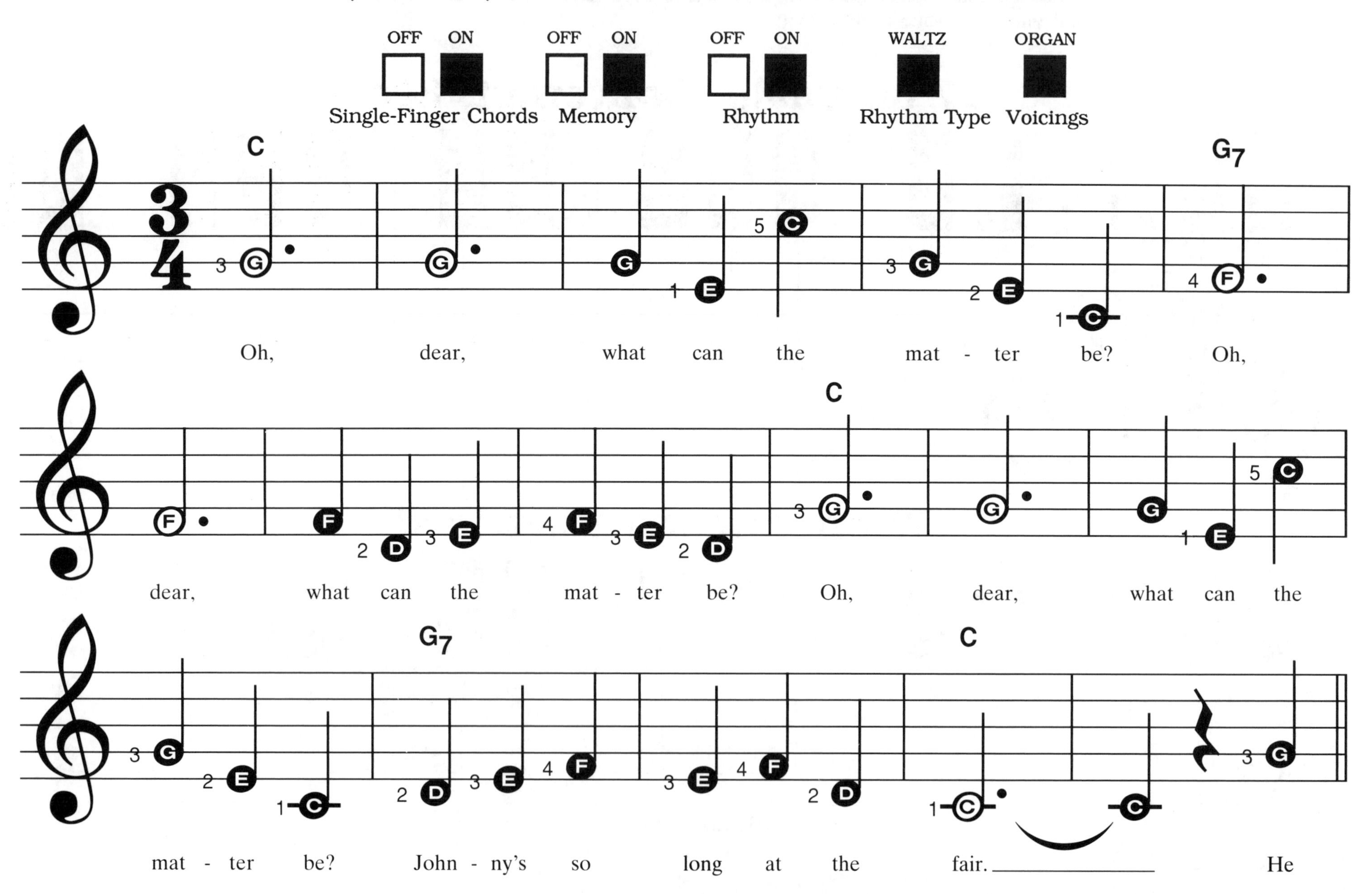

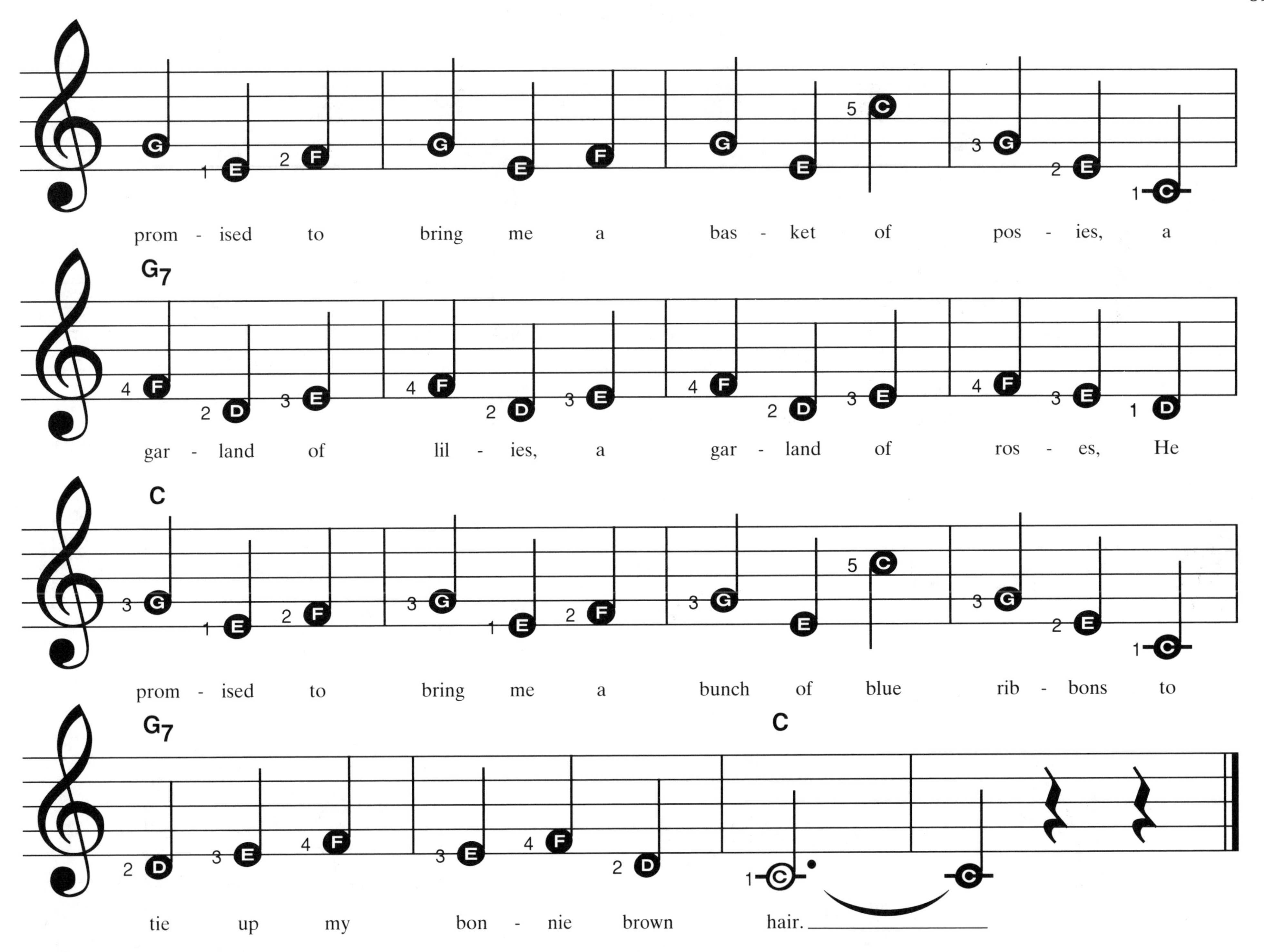

G E F G E F G E C G E C
prom - ised to bring me a bas - ket of pos - ies, a
G7
F D E F D E F D E F E D
gar - land of lil - ies, a gar - land of ros - es, He
C
G E F G E F G E C G E C
prom - ised to bring me a bunch of blue rib - bons to
G7
C
D E F E F D C C
tie up my bon - nie brown hair.

Marianne

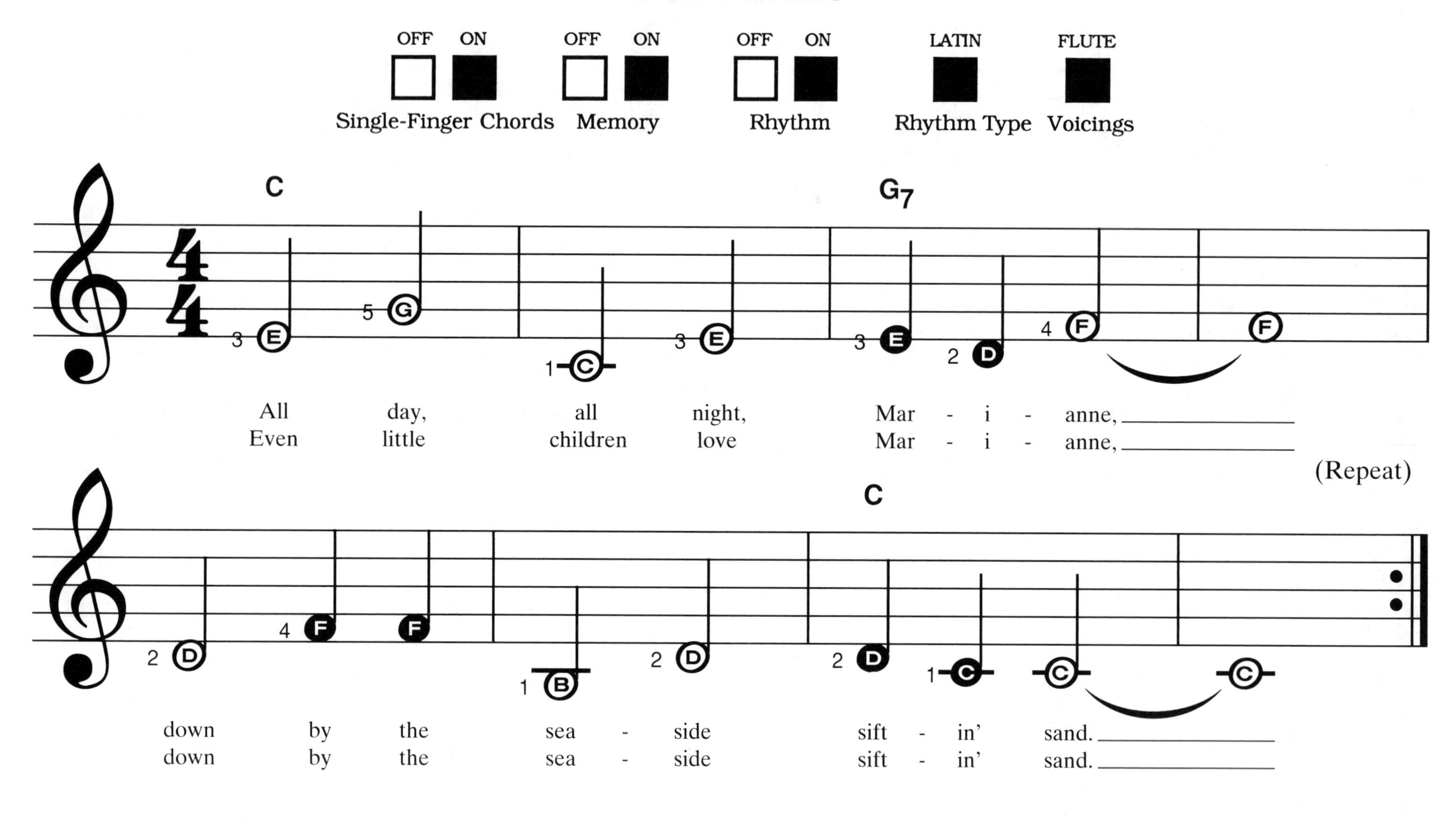

Eighth-Note Rest

An eight-note rest receives the same time value as an eighth note.

He's Got the Whole World in His Hands

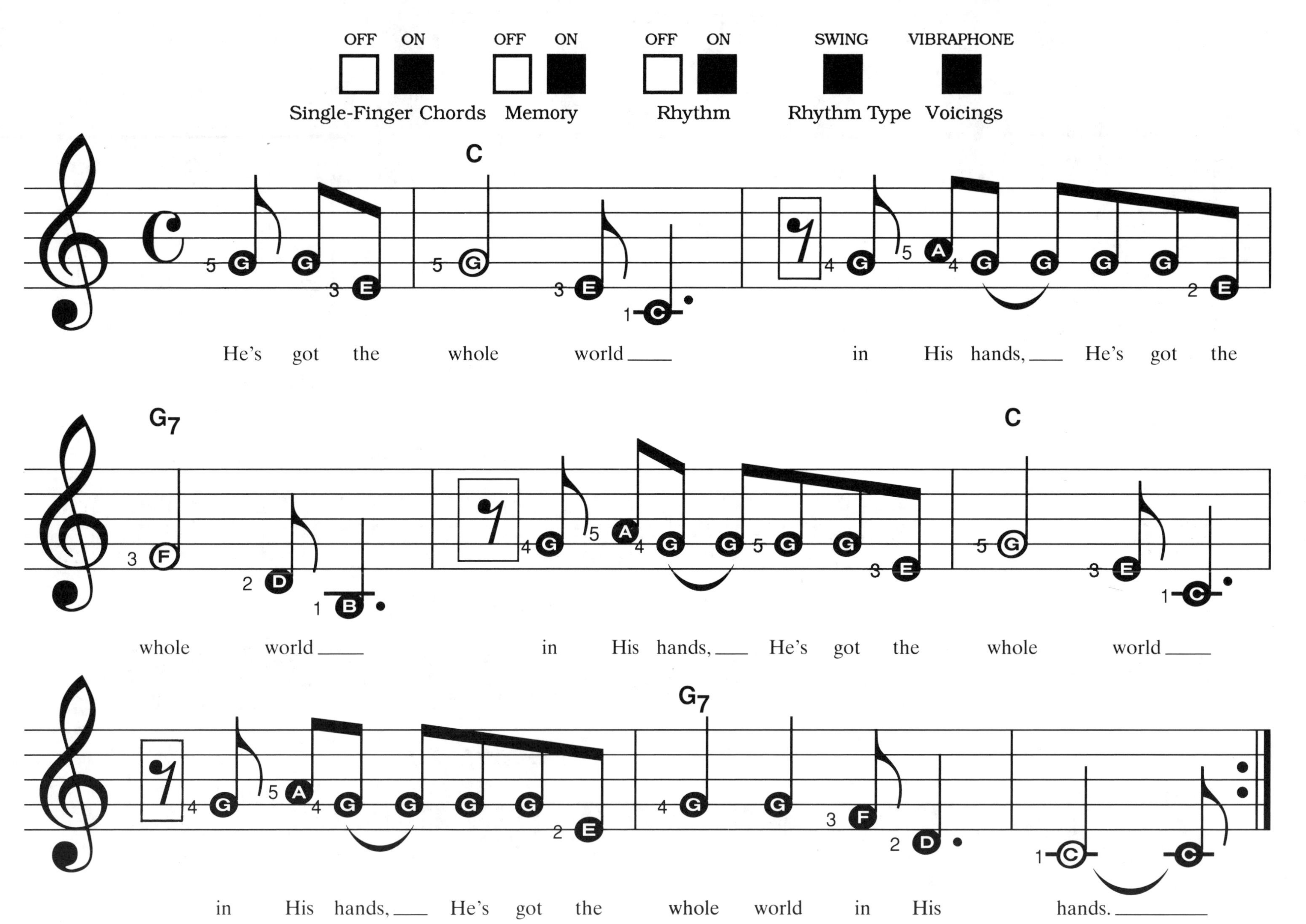

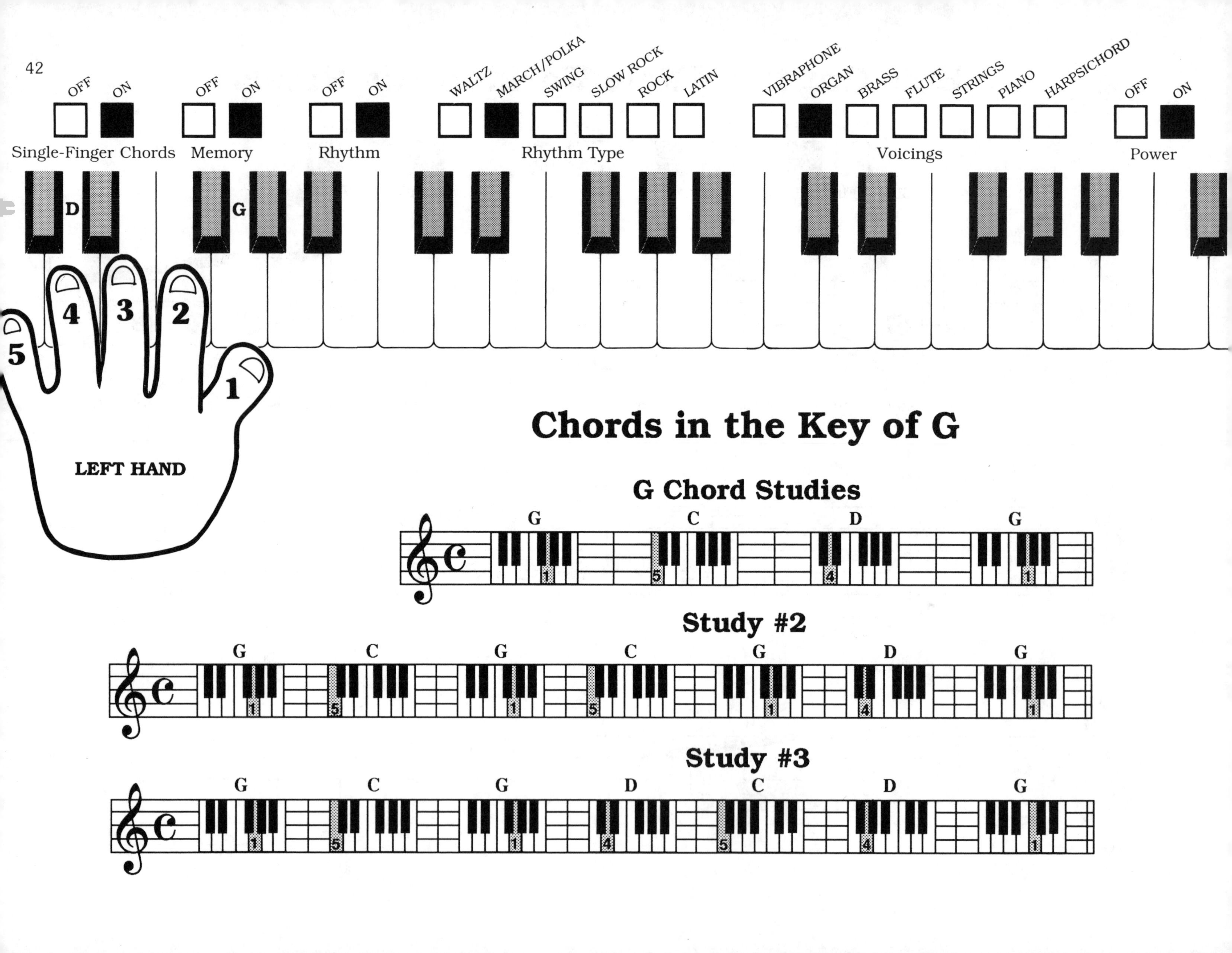

Chords in the Key of G

G Chord Studies

Study #2

Study #3

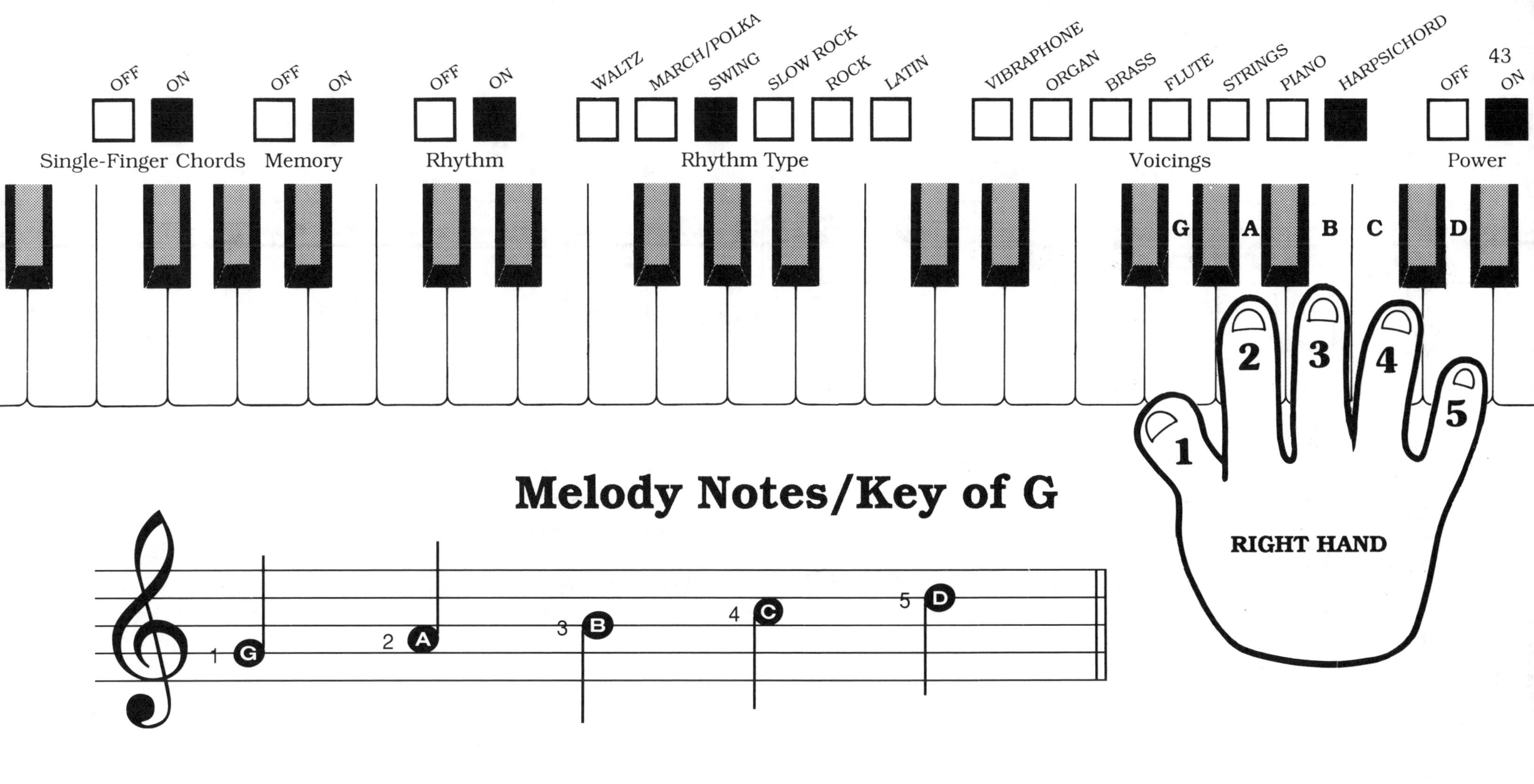

Melody Notes/Key of G

Mama Don't 'Low

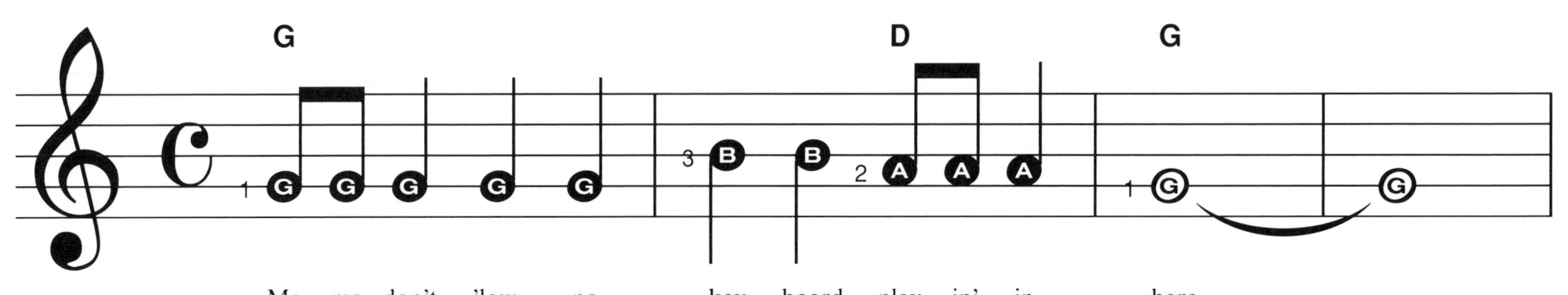

Ma - ma don't 'low no key - board play - in' in here, ________

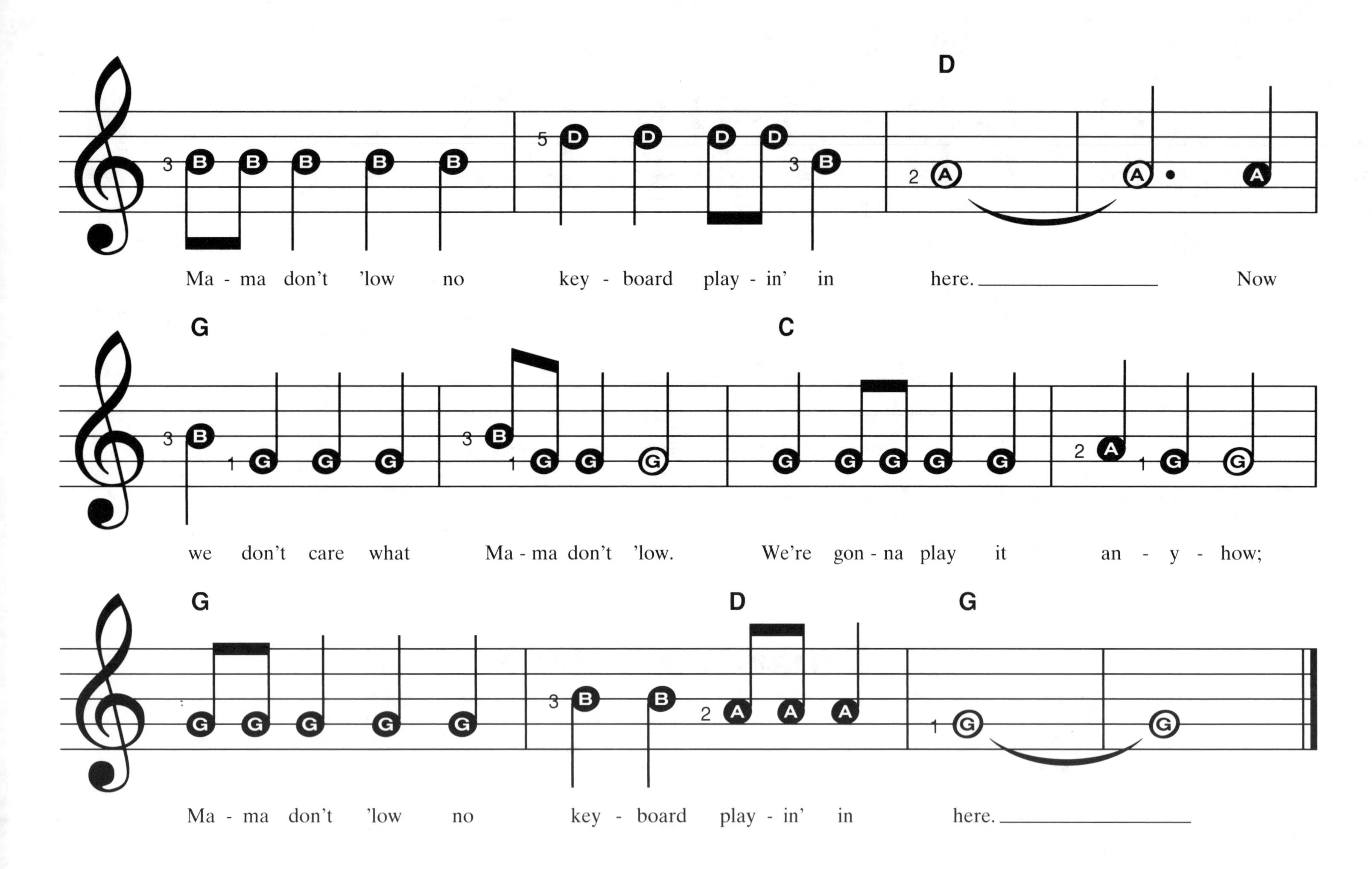
D
Ma - ma don't 'low no key - board play - in' in here. Now
G
C
we don't care what Ma - ma don't 'low. We're gon - na play it an - y - how;
G
D
G
Ma - ma don't 'low no key - board play - in' in here.

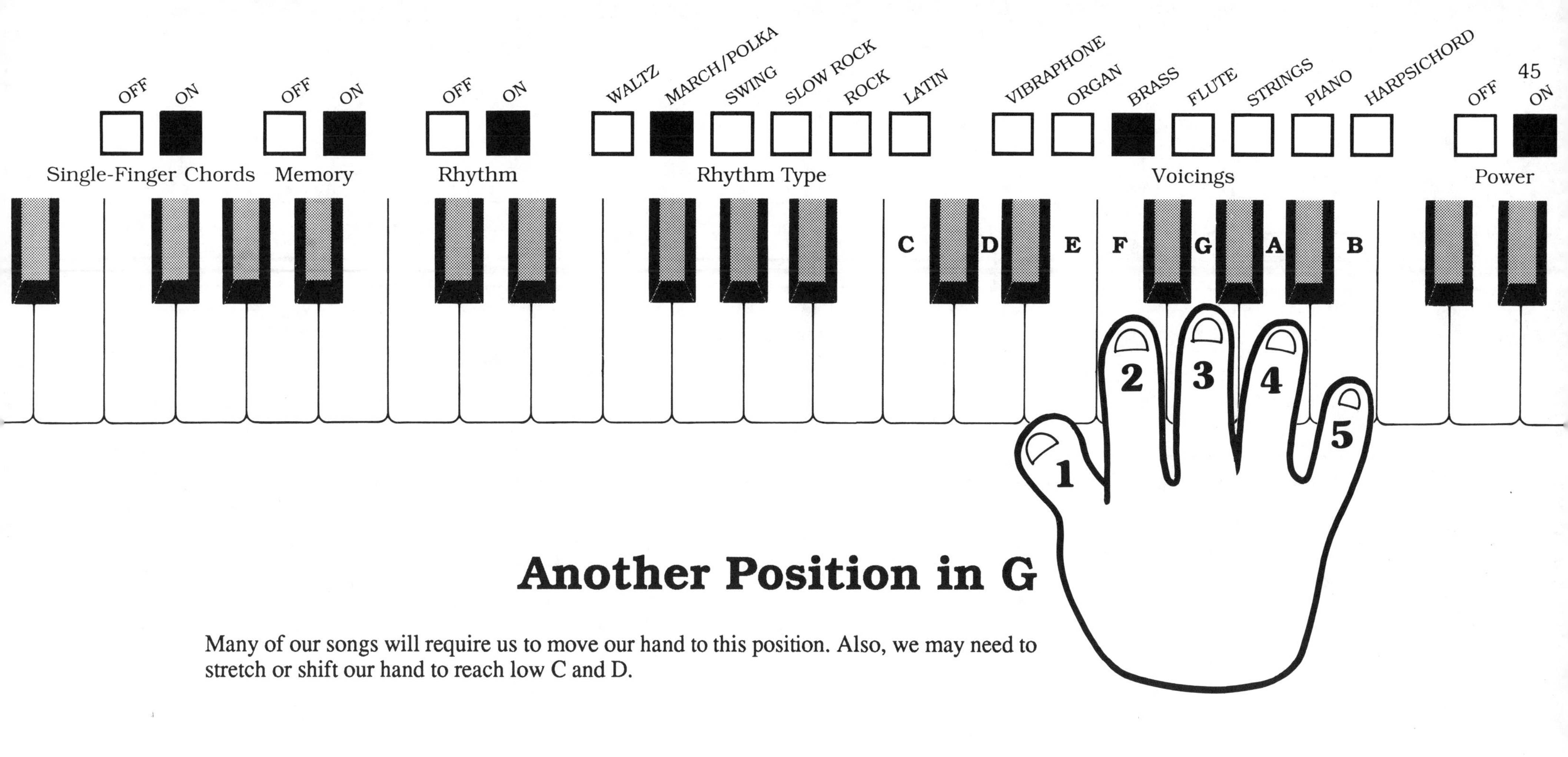

Another Position in G

Many of our songs will require us to move our hand to this position. Also, we may need to stretch or shift our hand to reach low C and D.

Our Boys Will Shine Tonight

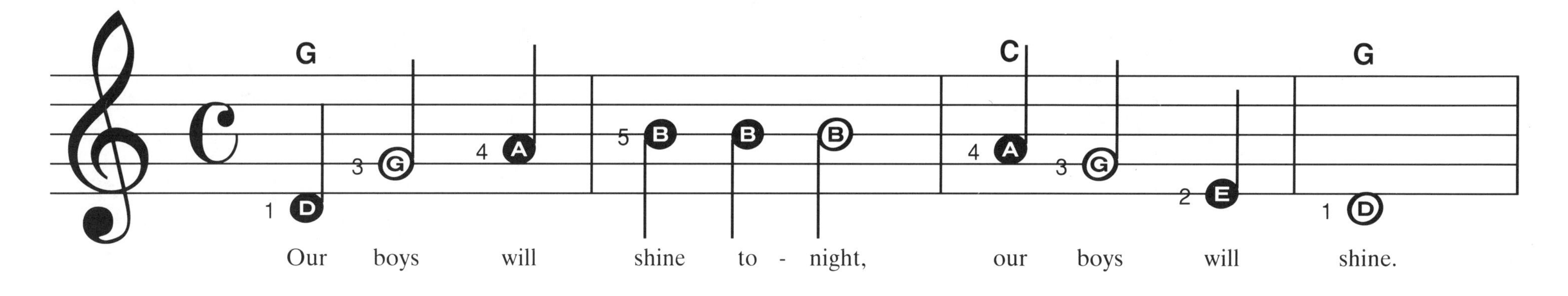

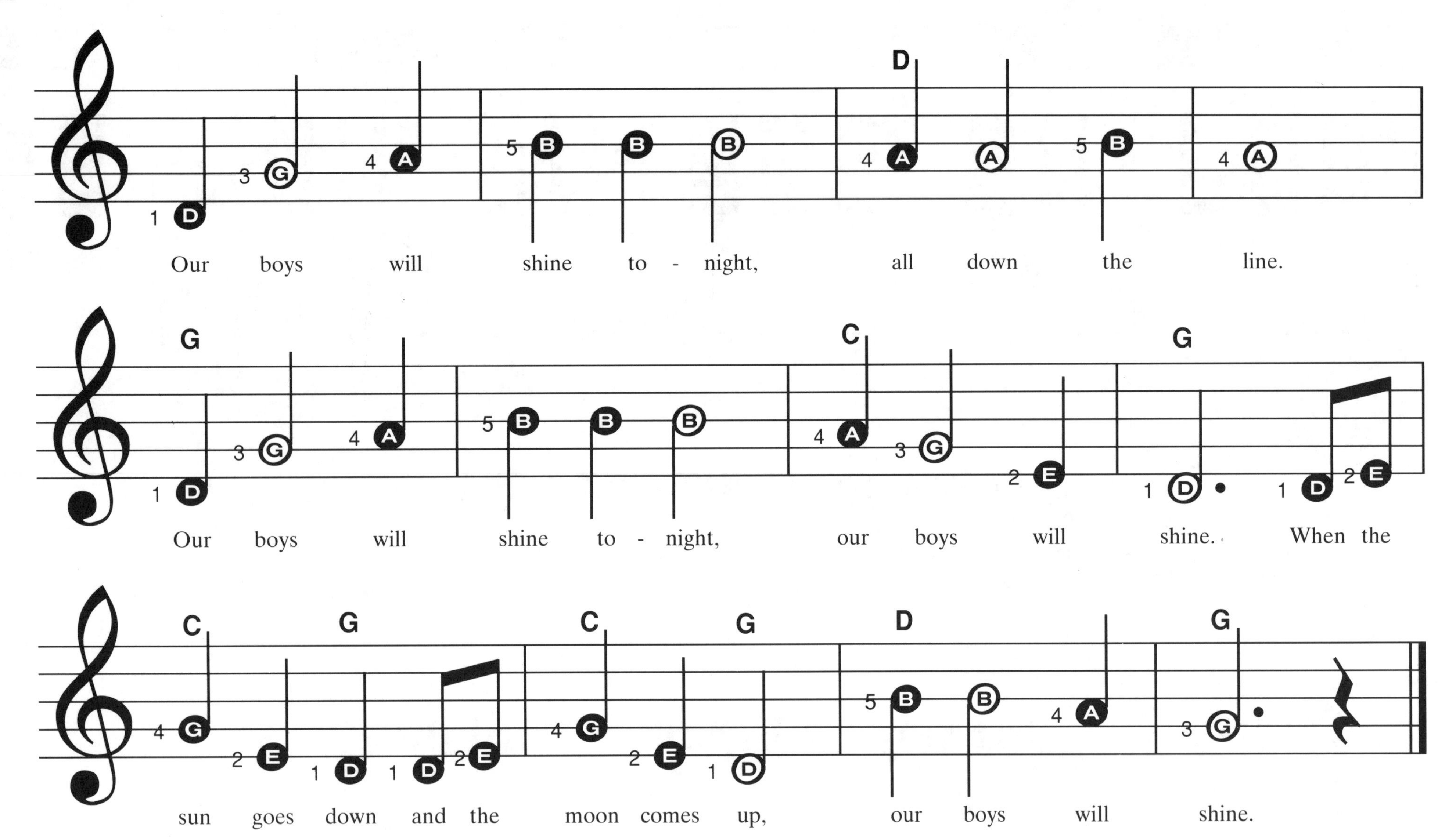
D
Our boys will shine to - night, all down the line.
G C G
Our boys will shine to - night, our boys will shine. When the
C G C G D G
sun goes down and the moon comes up, our boys will shine.

Amazing Grace

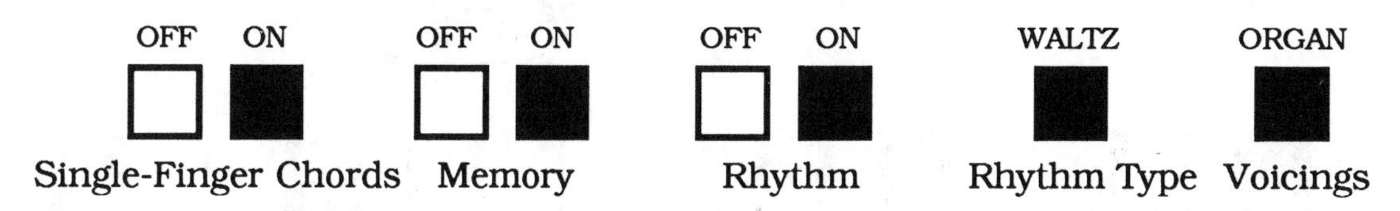

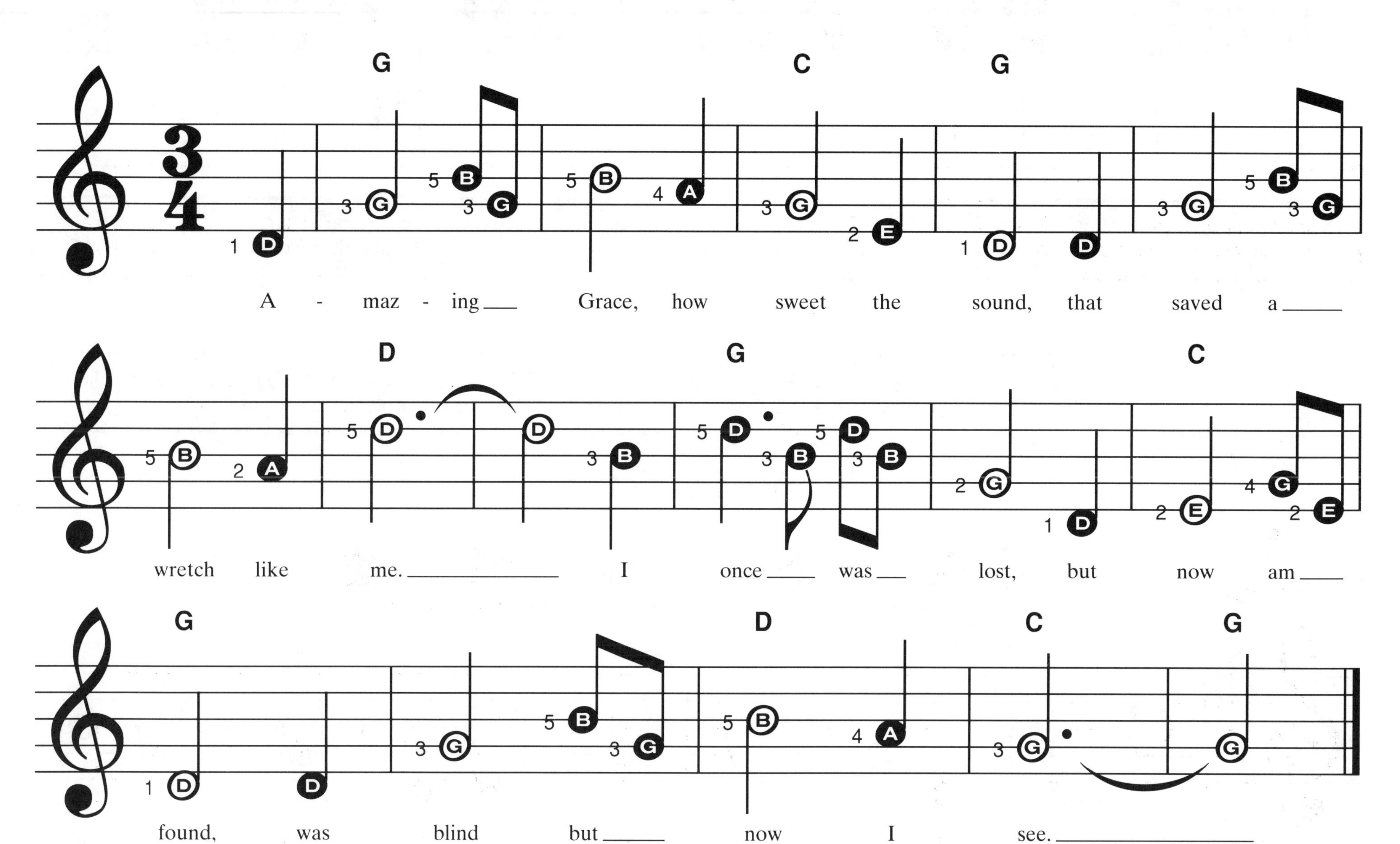

Sharps/F♯

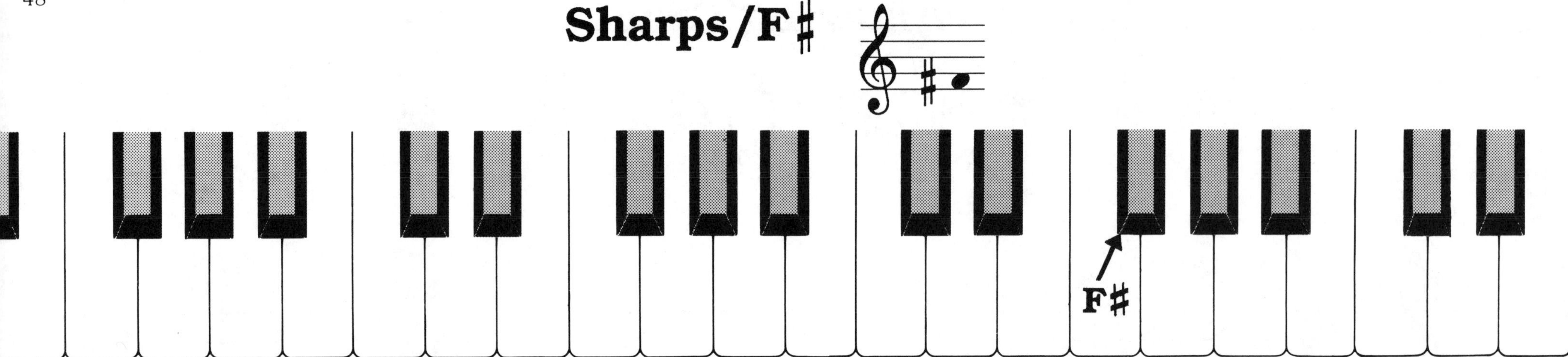

A sharp sign looks like this ♯. When placed in front of a note, it means to raise that note one half step. On your keyboard, a sharp sign in front of a note means to play the next key (black or white) to the *right* of the sharped note. With F♯, we play the first *black* key to the right of F.

Key Signature

When one sharp appears at the left of each line of music, then you have one sharp in the key signature. When this occurs, you are in the "key of G," and *all* F♯'s will be played as F♯ unless there is a natural sign ♮ in front of the F. A natural sign cancels out the sharp (♮).

Blow, Ye Winds

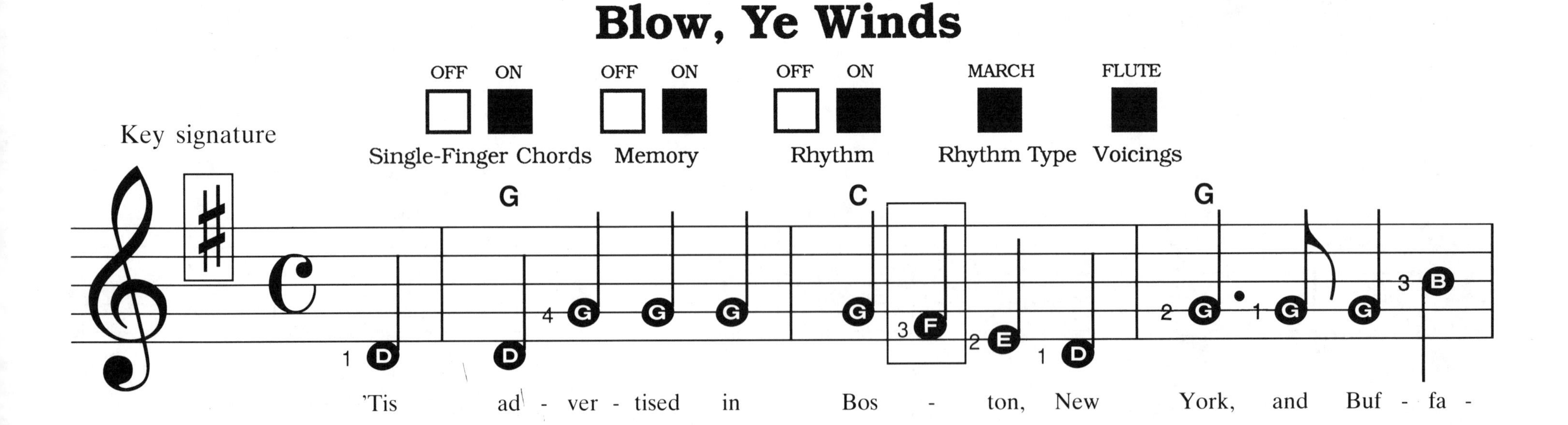

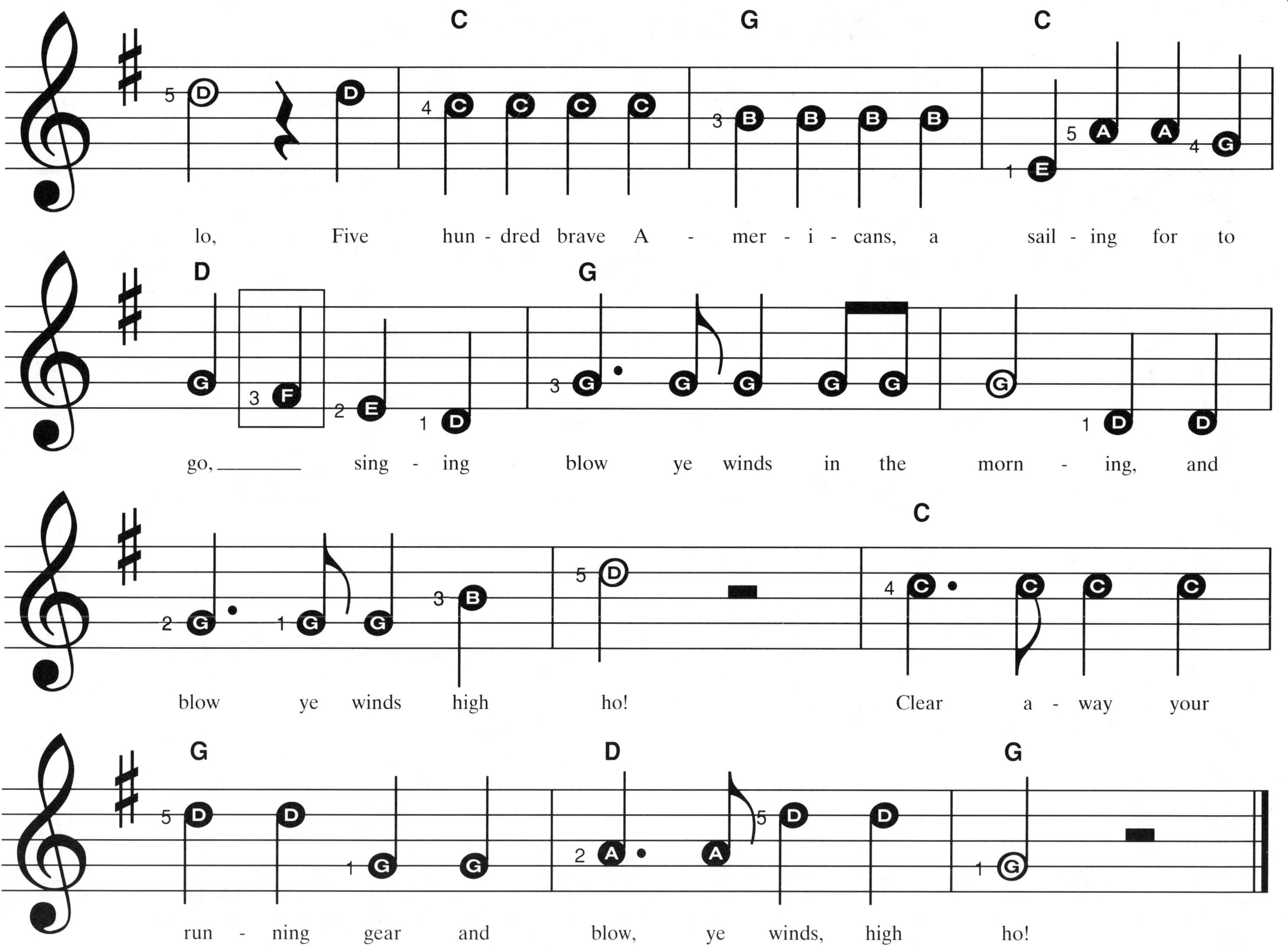
C G C
lo, Five hun - dred brave A - mer - i - cans, a sail - ing for to
D G
go, sing - ing blow ye winds in the morn - ing, and
C
blow ye winds high ho! Clear a - way your
G D G
run - ning gear and blow, ye winds, high ho!

This Little Light of Mine

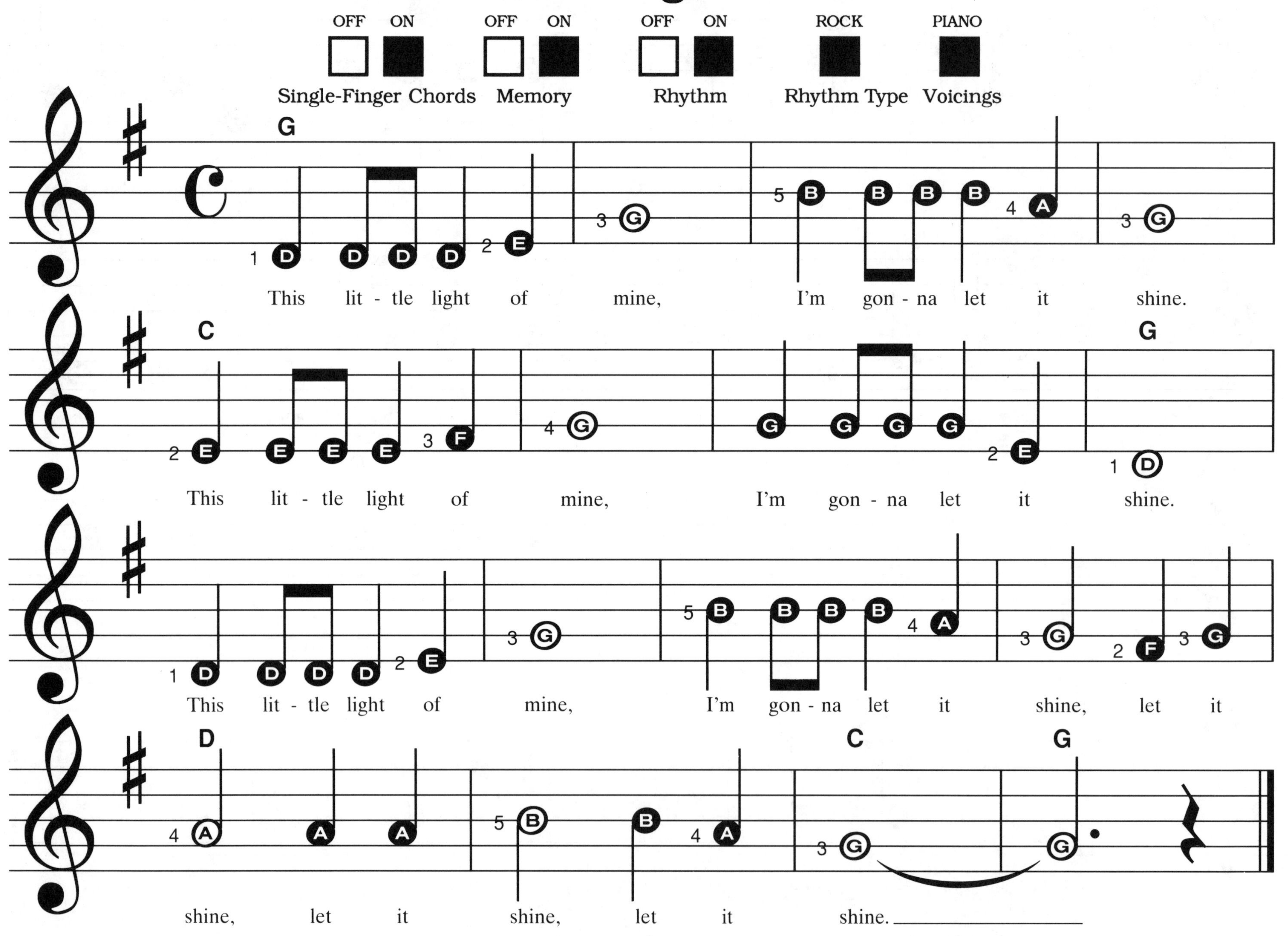

D7 Chord

Casio & Bontempi

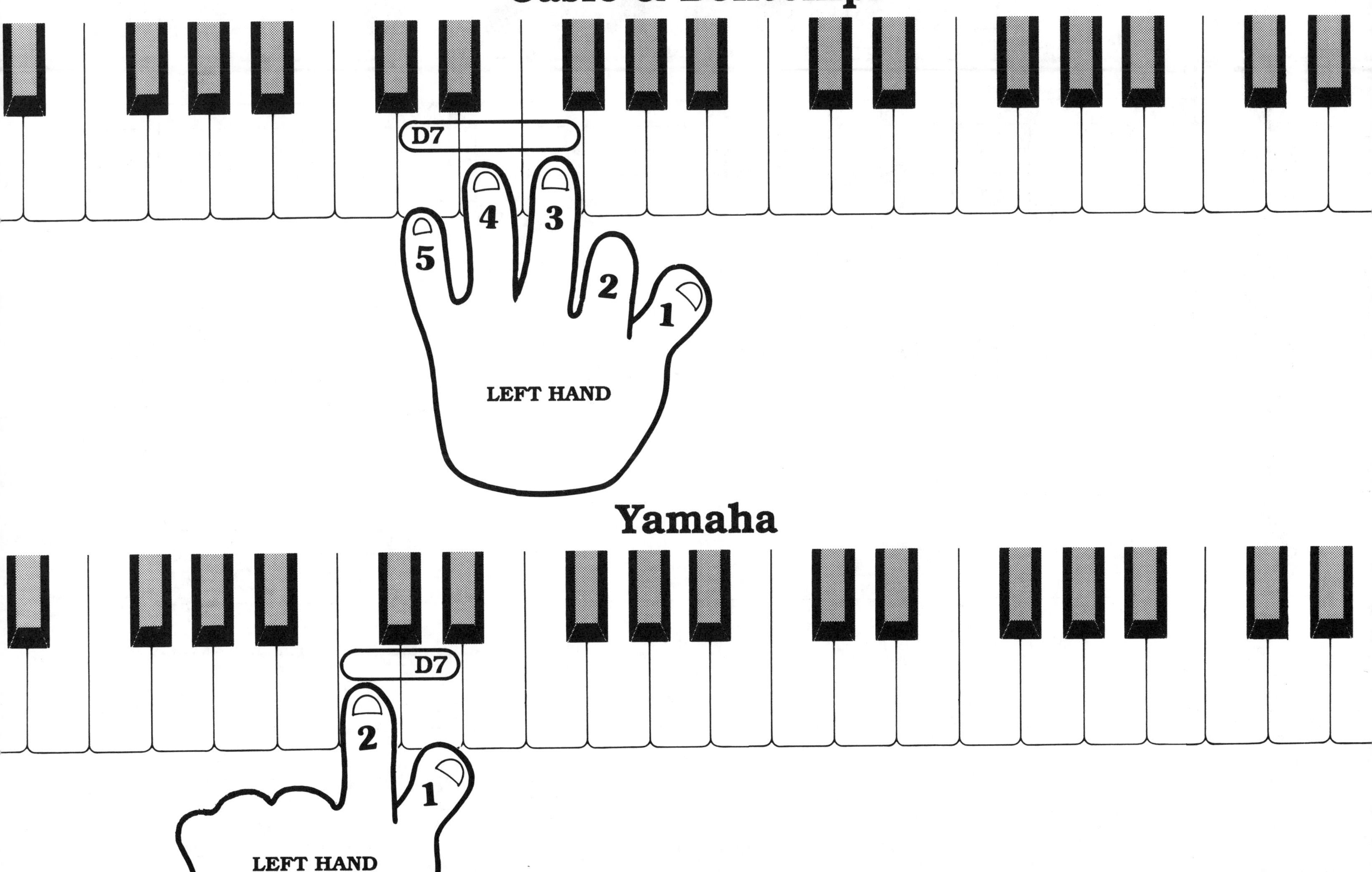

She'll Be Comin' 'Round the Mountain

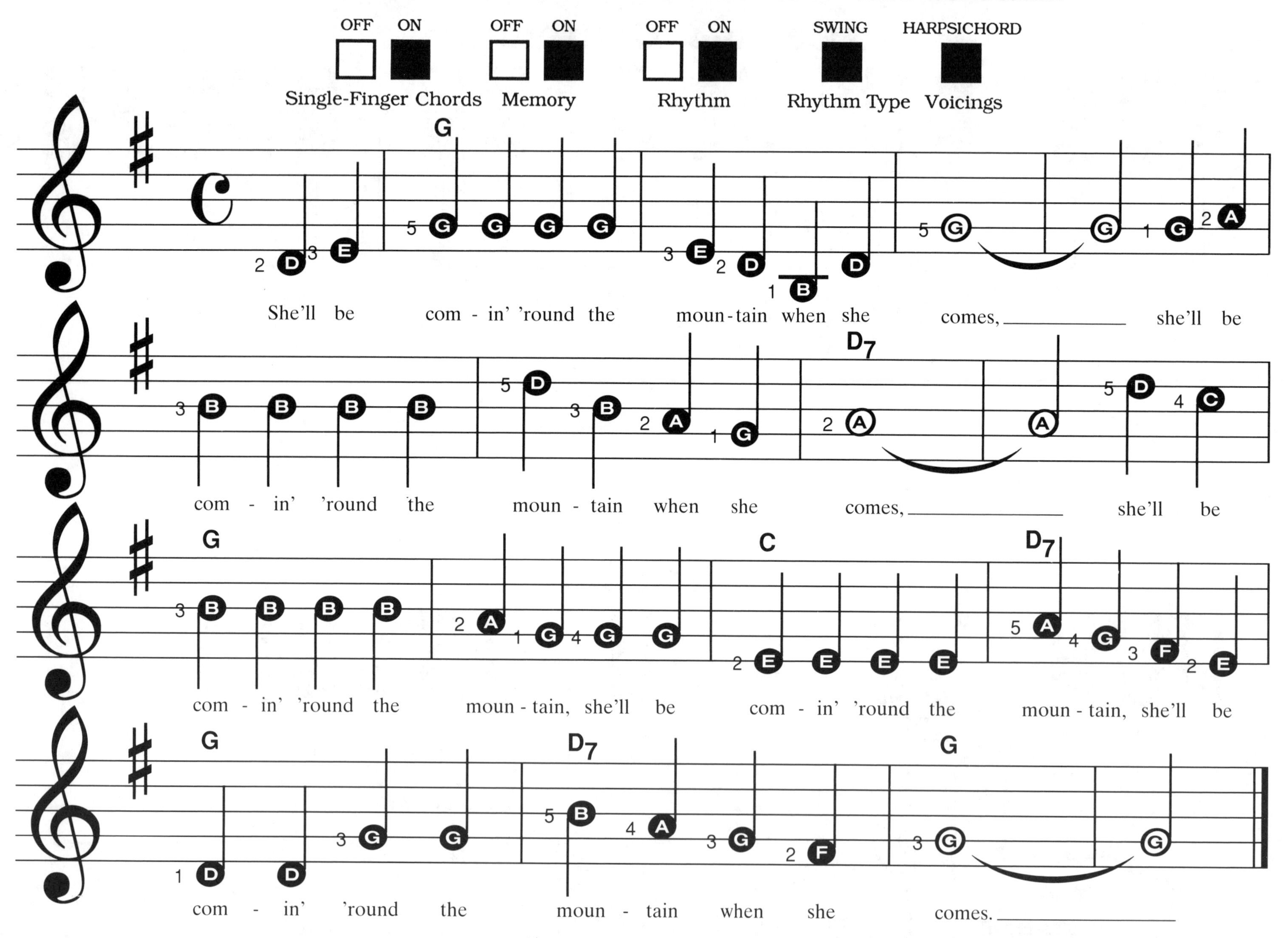

Red River Valley

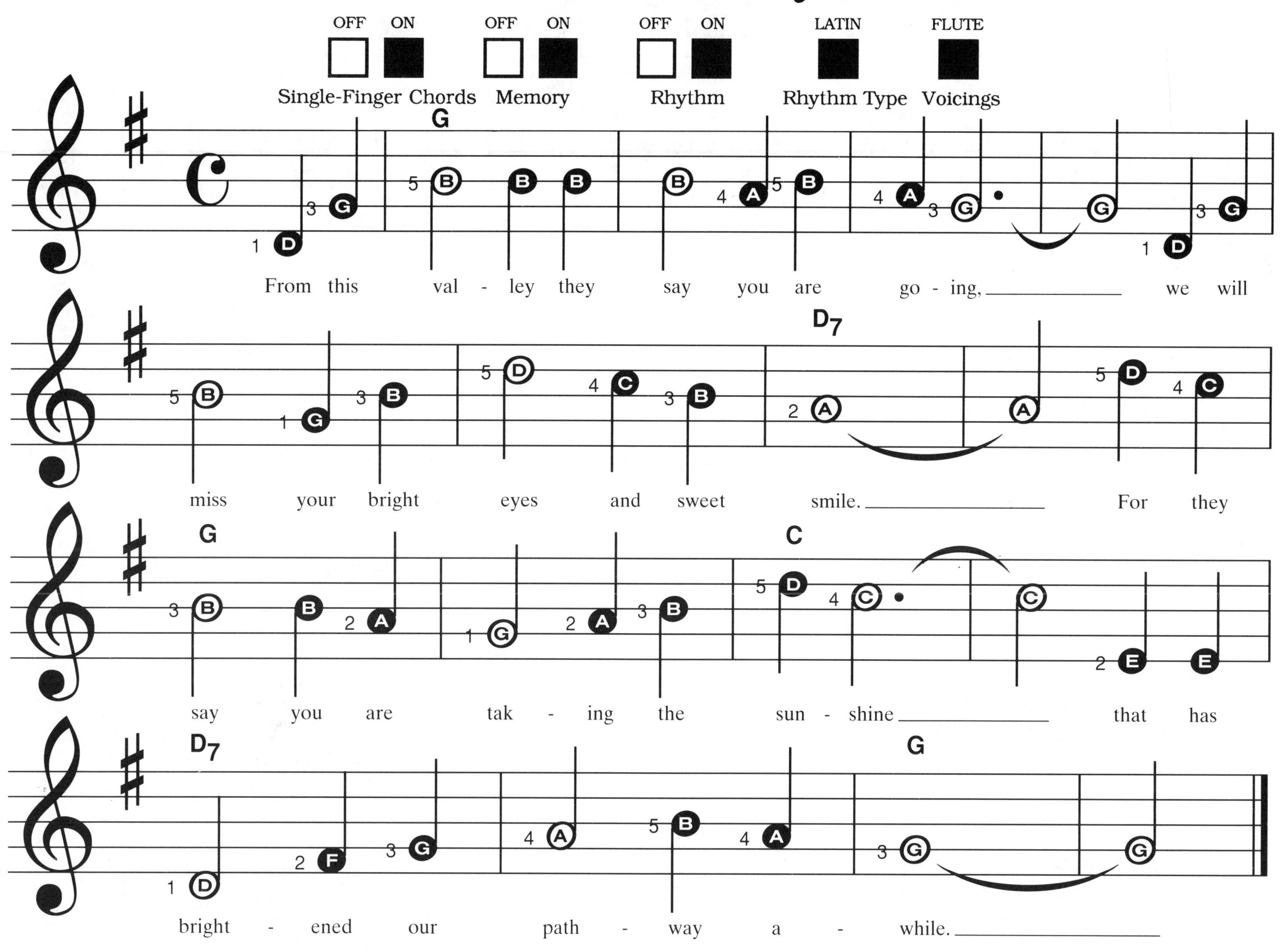

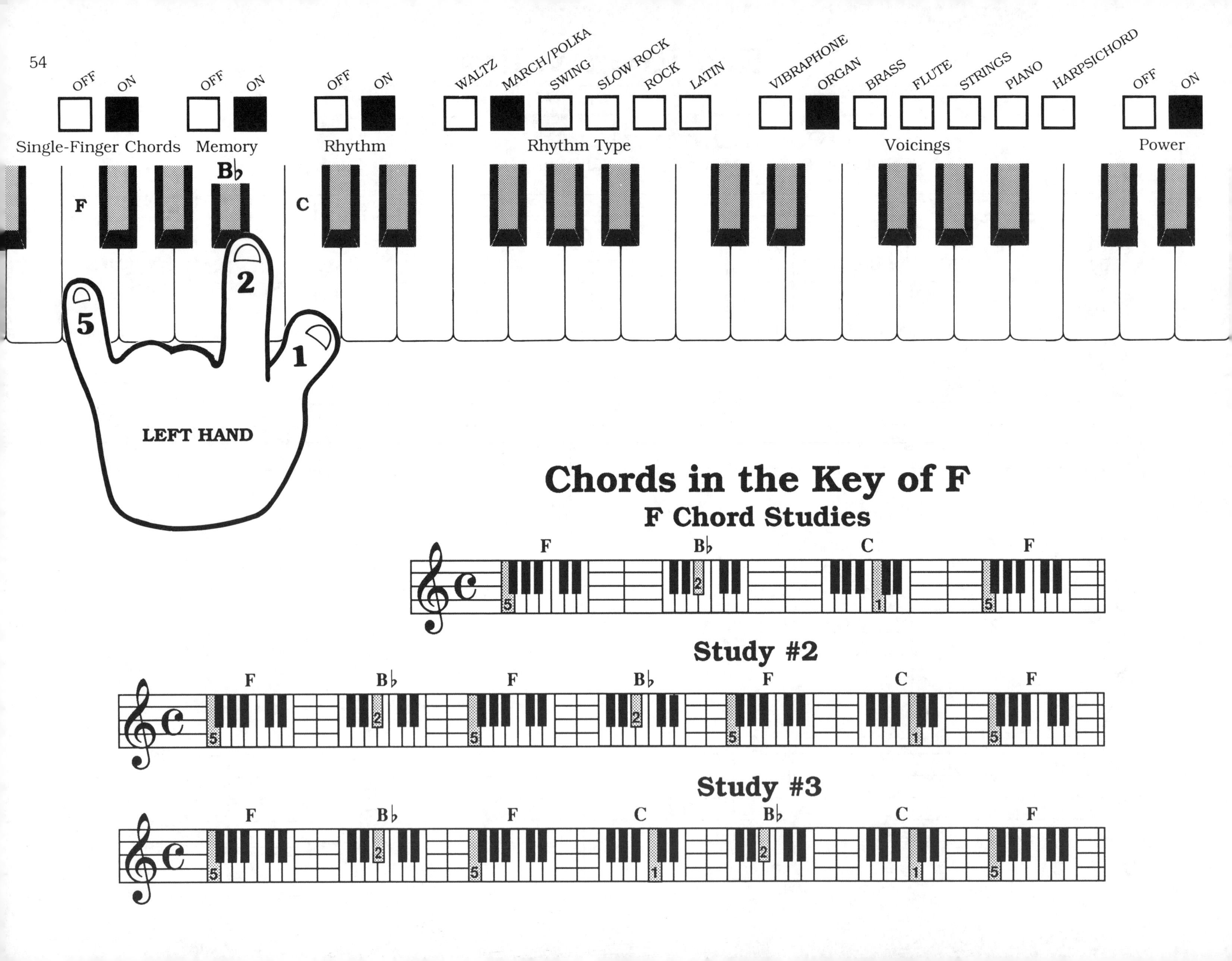

Chords in the Key of F

F Chord Studies

Study #2

Study #3

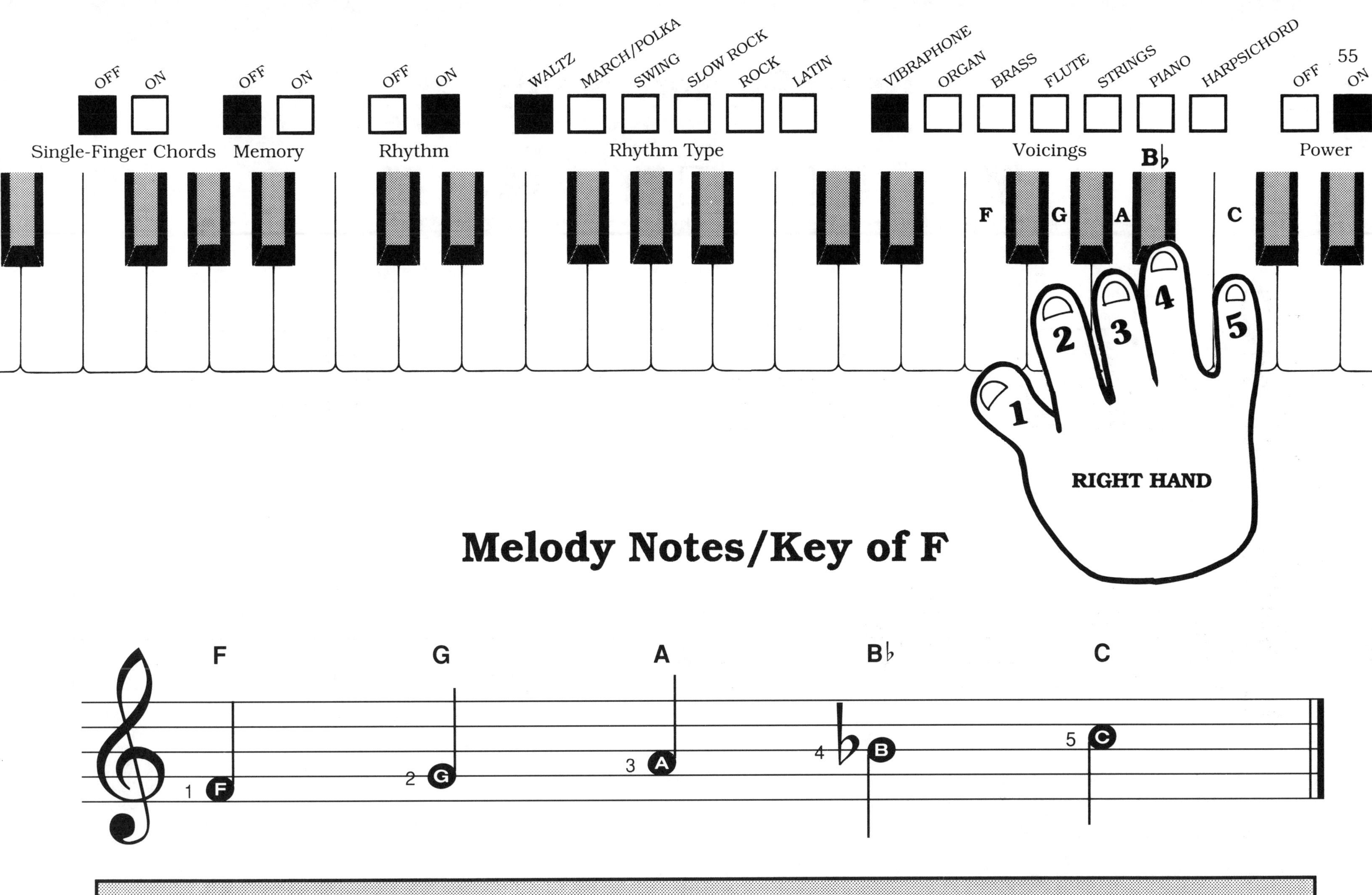

Melody Notes/Key of F

A flat sign looks like this ♭. When placed in front of a note, it means to lower that note one half step. On your keyboard, a flat sign in front of a note means to play the next key (black or white) to the *left* of the flatted note. A natural sign ♮ cancels out a flat. This key signature [treble clef with one flat] means you are in the *key of F*.

Key-of-F Note Study

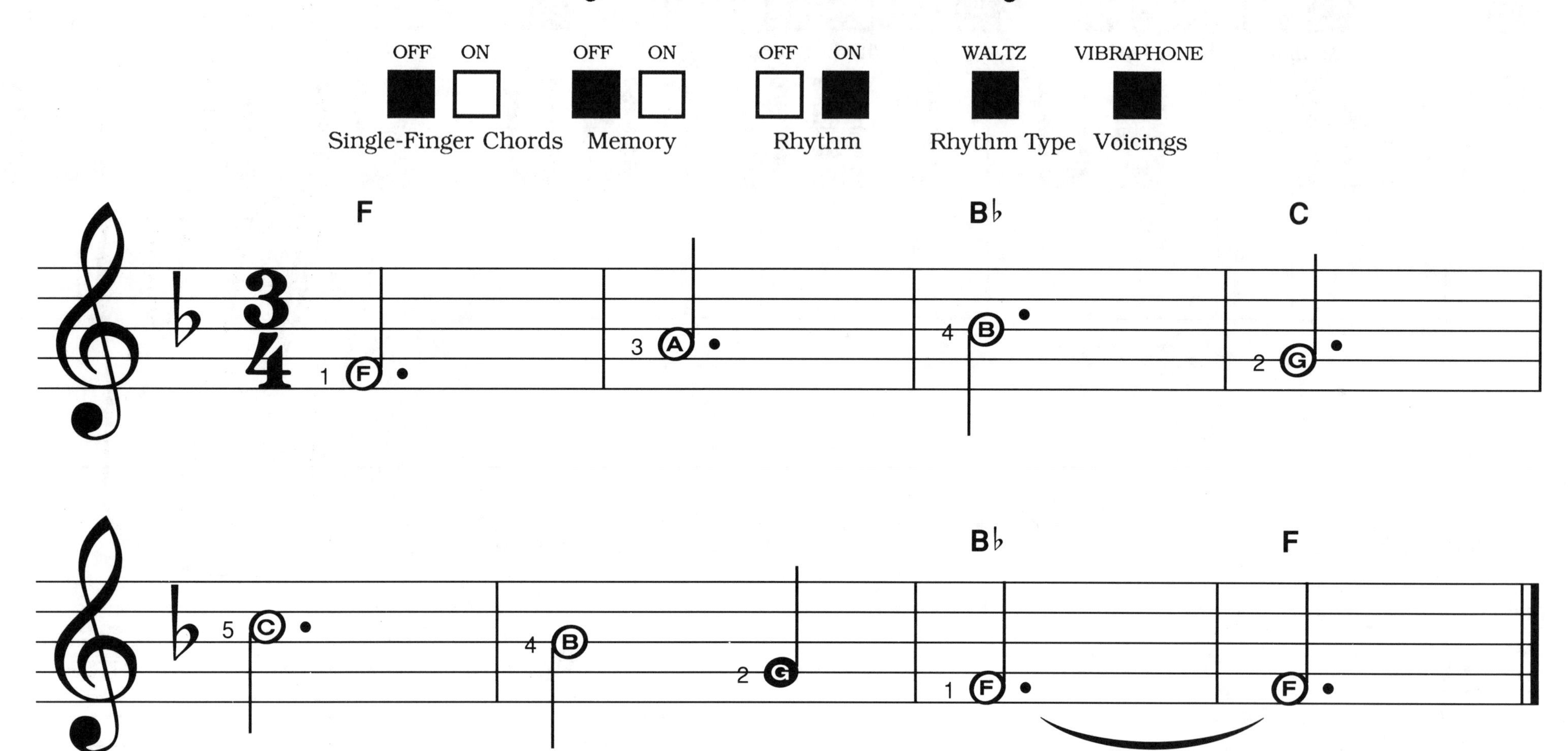

Yankee Doodle

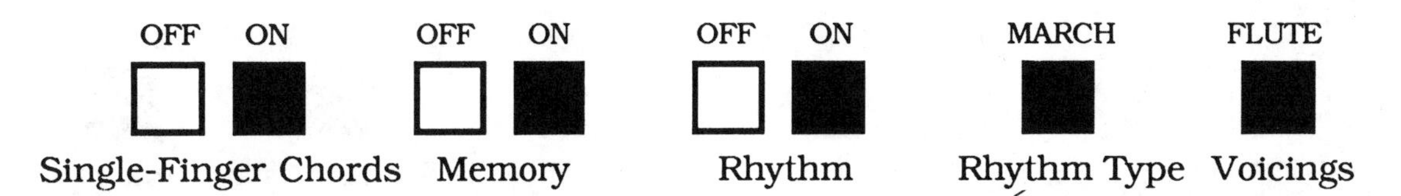

[Watch finger numbers to show shifts in right hand position.]

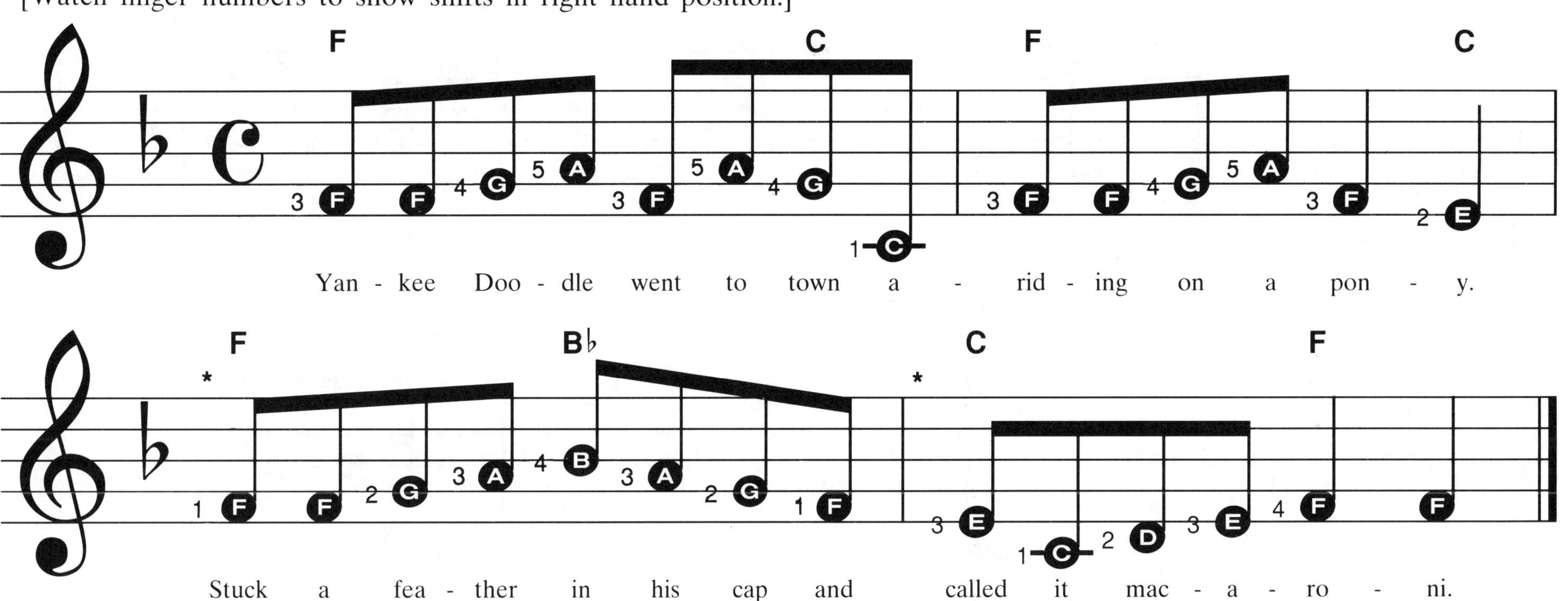

***Sometimes it is necessary to have a finger "cross over." This is the case here.**

John Jacob Jingleheimer Schmidt

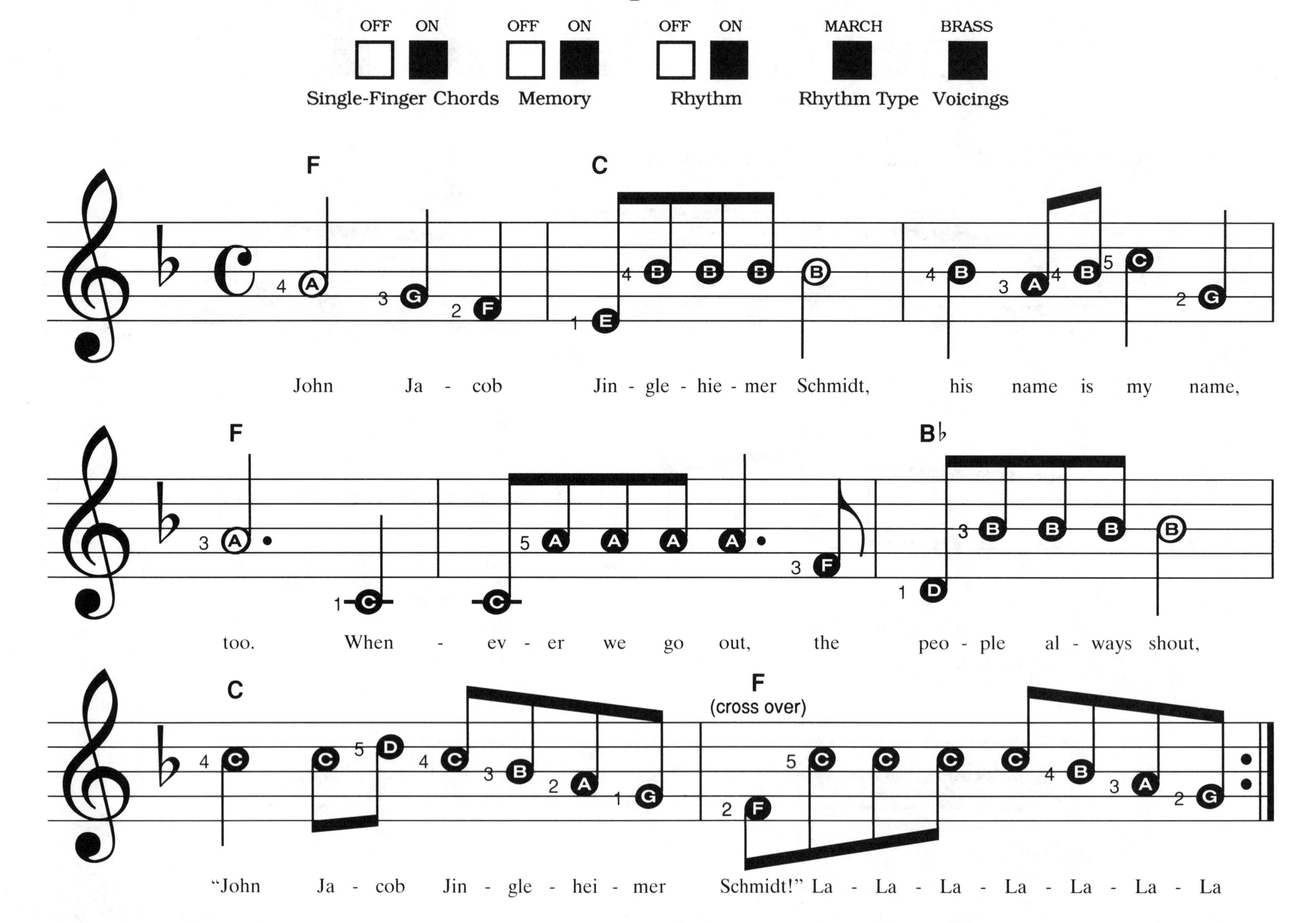

C7 Chord

Casio & Bontempi

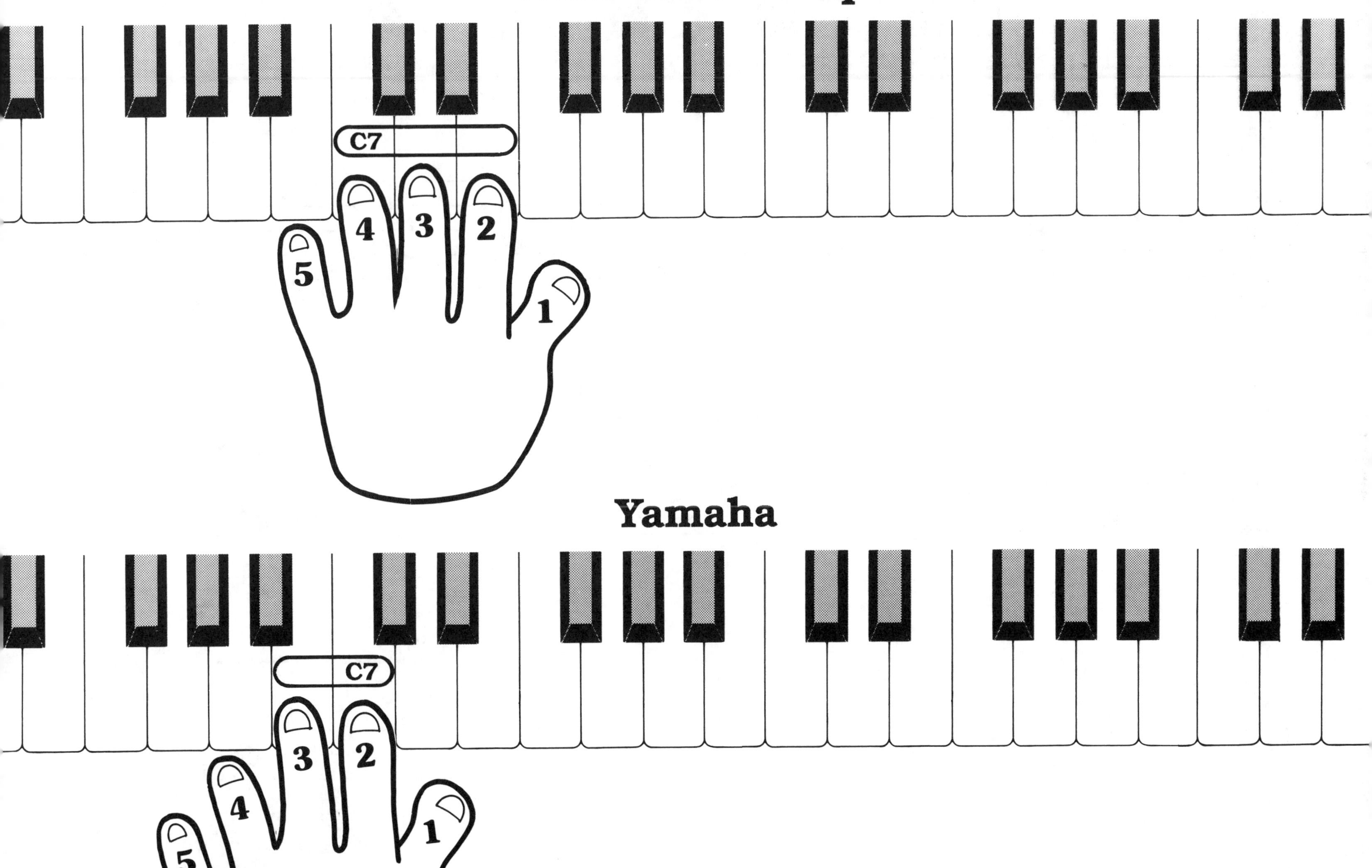

Sourwood Mountain

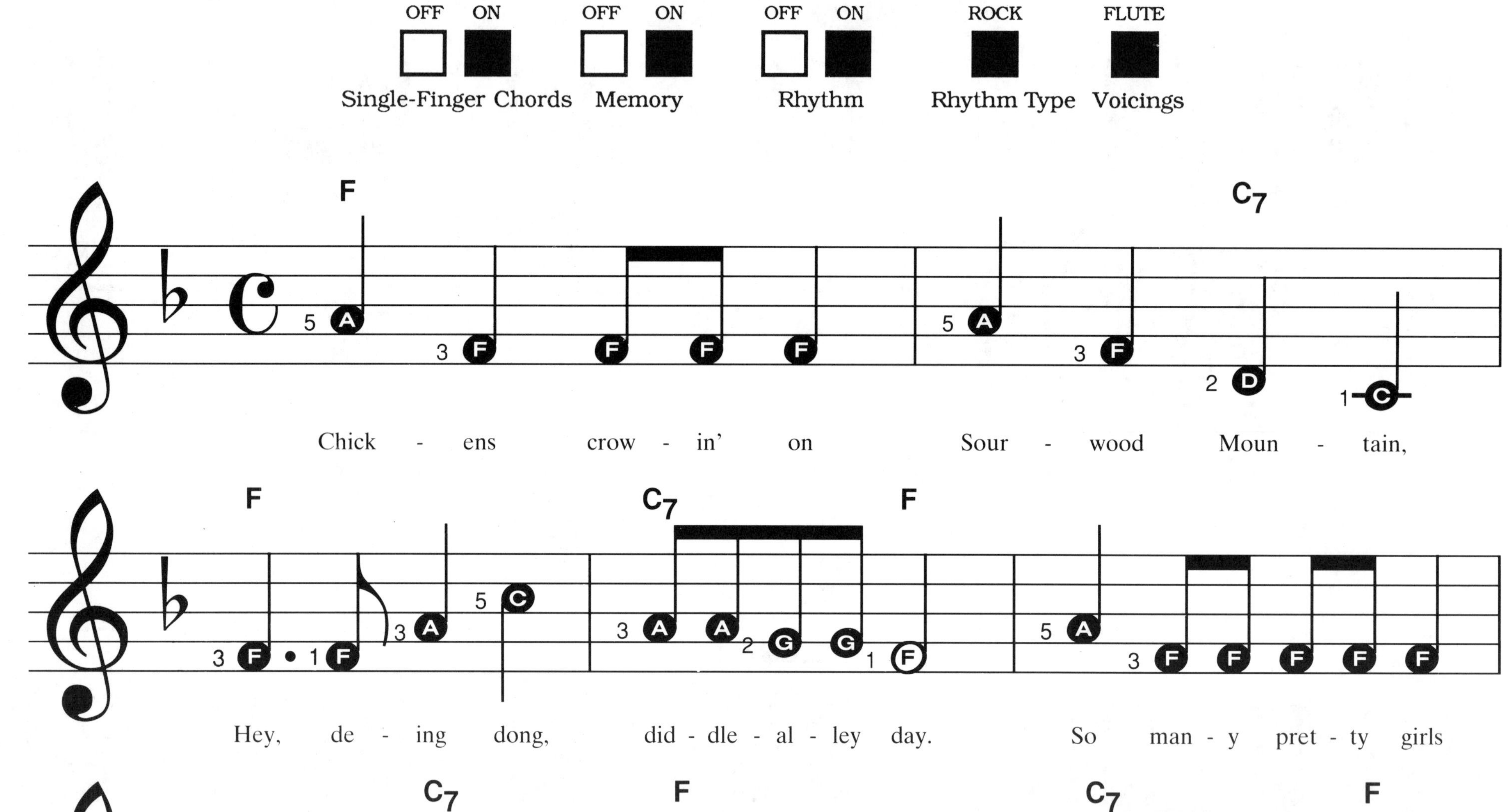

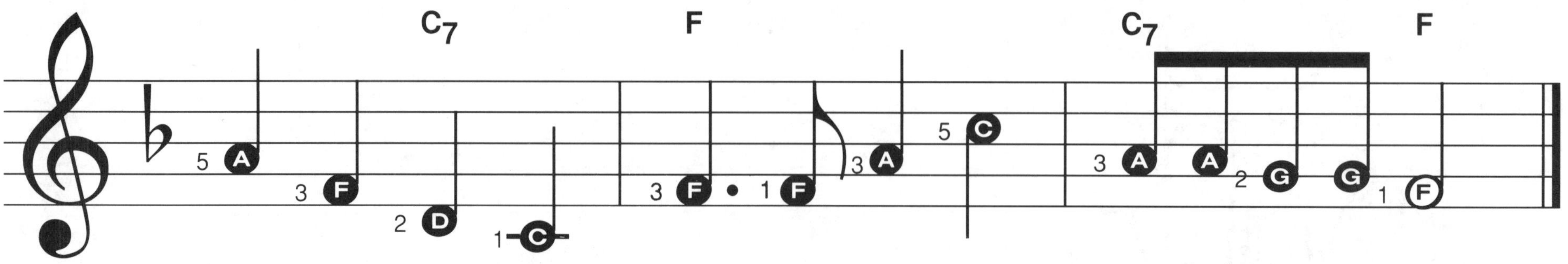

Down in the Valley

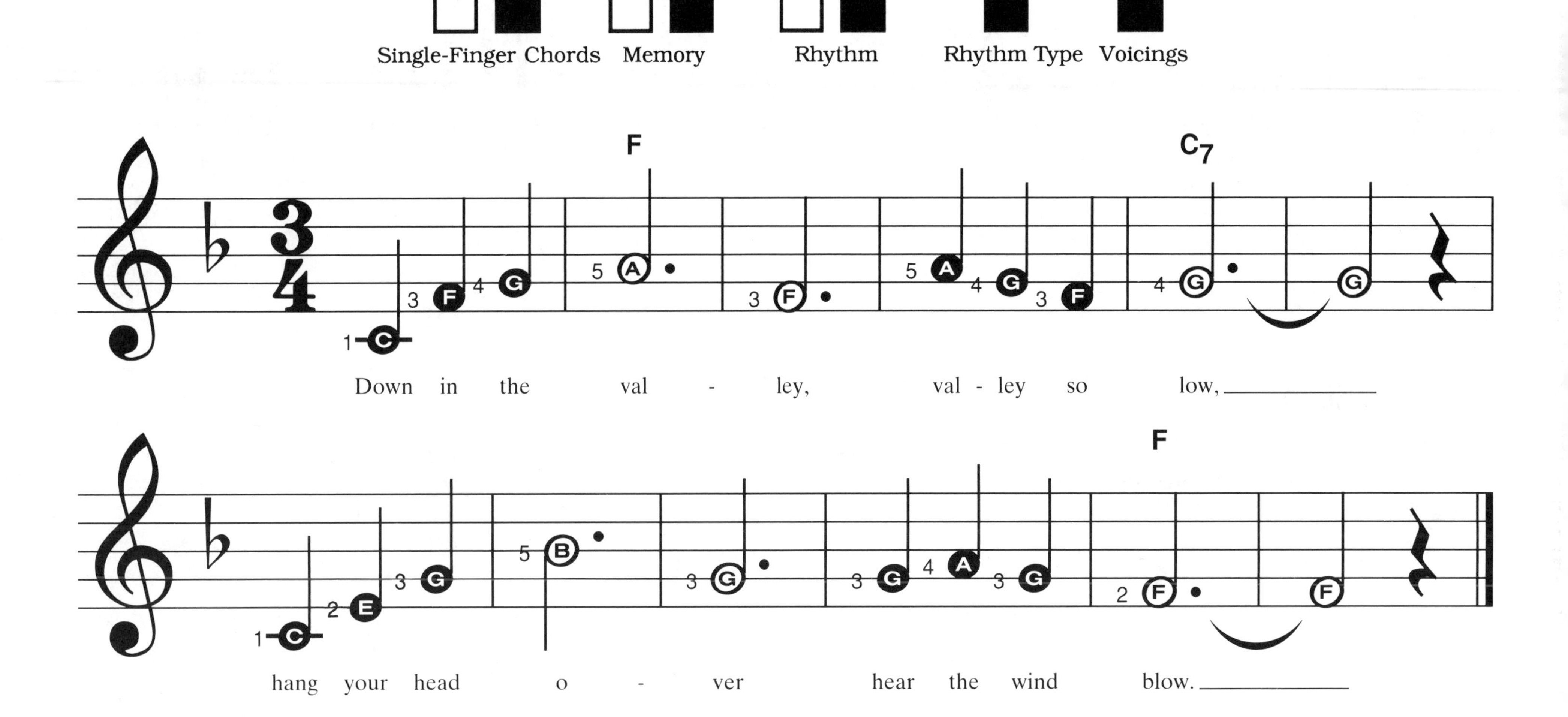

Vs. 2. Roses love sunshine, Violets love dew,
Angels in heaven know I love you.

3 New Notes

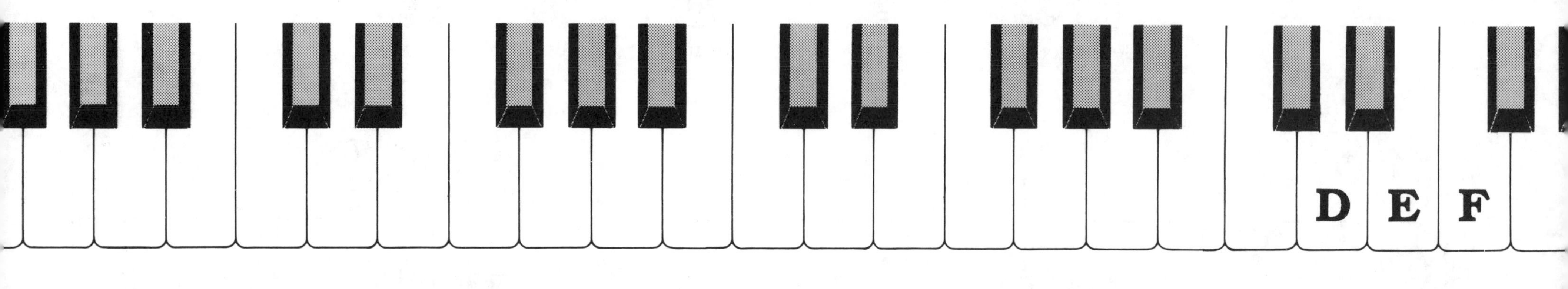

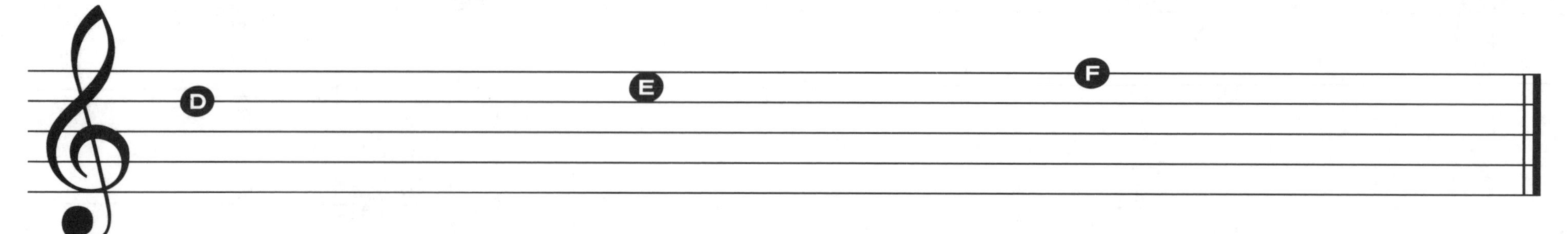

Fairest Lord Jesus

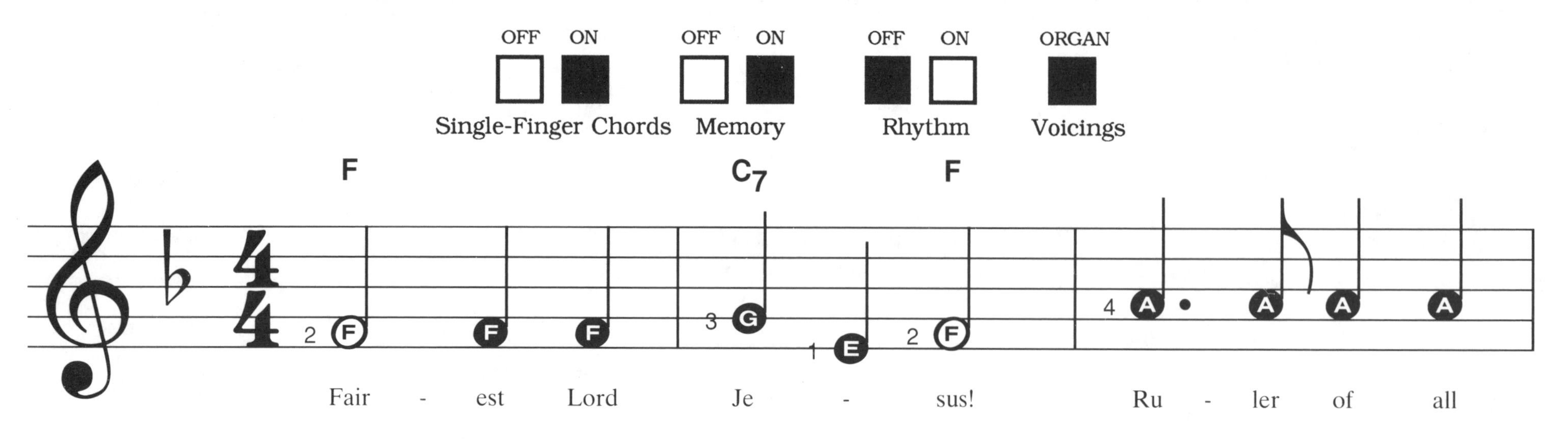

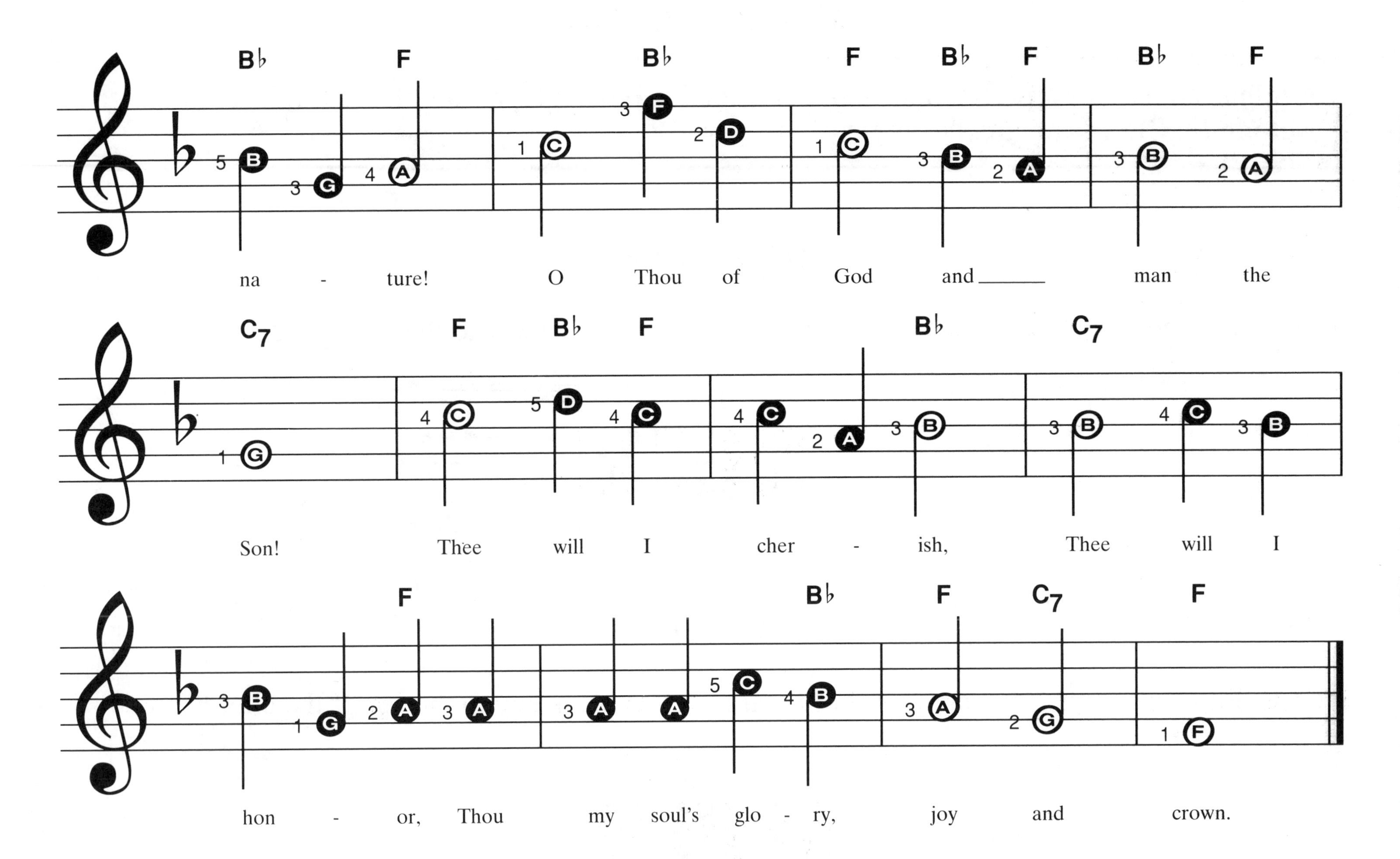
B♭ F B♭ F B♭ F B♭ F
na - ture! O Thou of God and ___ man the
C7 F B♭ F B♭ C7
Son! Thee will I cher - ish, Thee will I
F B♭ F C7 F
hon - or, Thou my soul's glo - ry, joy and crown.

Minor Chords

A minor chord has a pretty, somewhat sad sound. Here is how you play a minor chord with Automatic Chords or Single-Finger Chords.

Casio/Bontempi

RULE: Play note with same name as chord *and* play next white key to the *right* of the chord note.

Dm

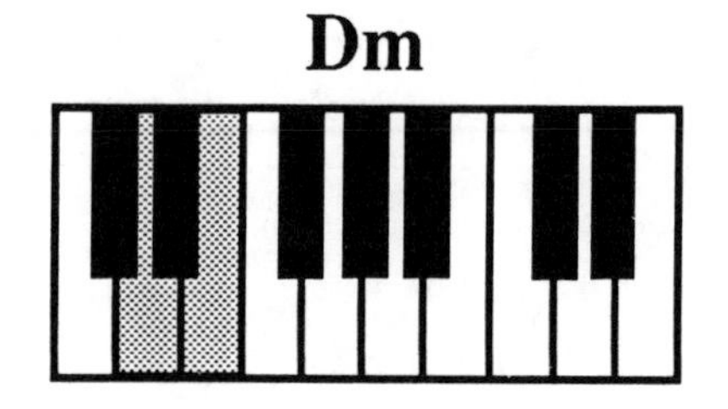

Yamaha

RULE: Play note with same name as chord *and* play first black key to the *left* of the chord note.

Dm

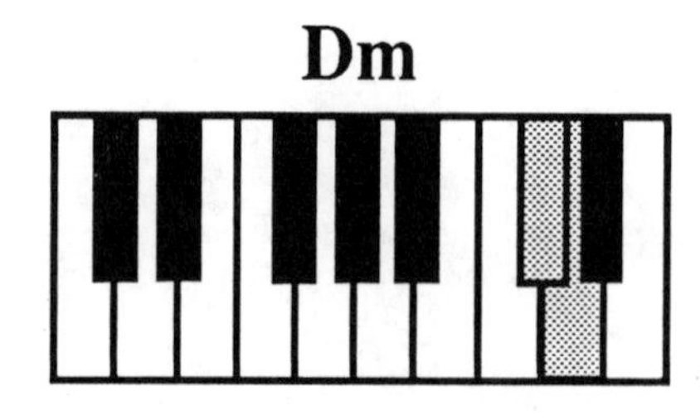

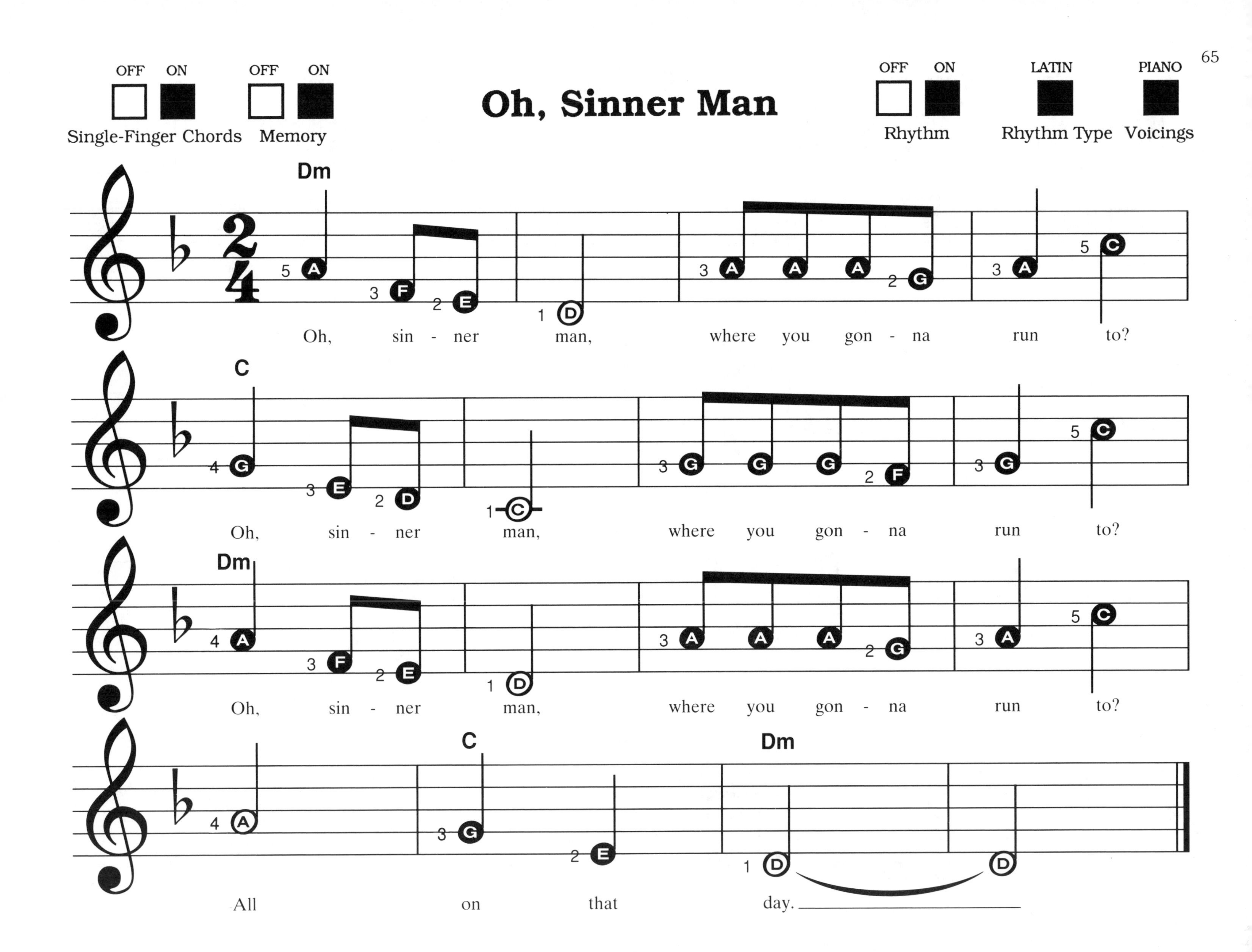
OFF ON
Single-Finger Chords
OFF ON
Memory
Oh, Sinner Man
OFF ON
Rhythm
LATIN
Rhythm Type
PIANO
Voicings
Dm
Oh, sin - ner man, where you gon - na run to?
C
Oh, sin - ner man, where you gon - na run to?
Dm
Oh, sin - ner man, where you gon - na run to?
C
Dm
All on that day.

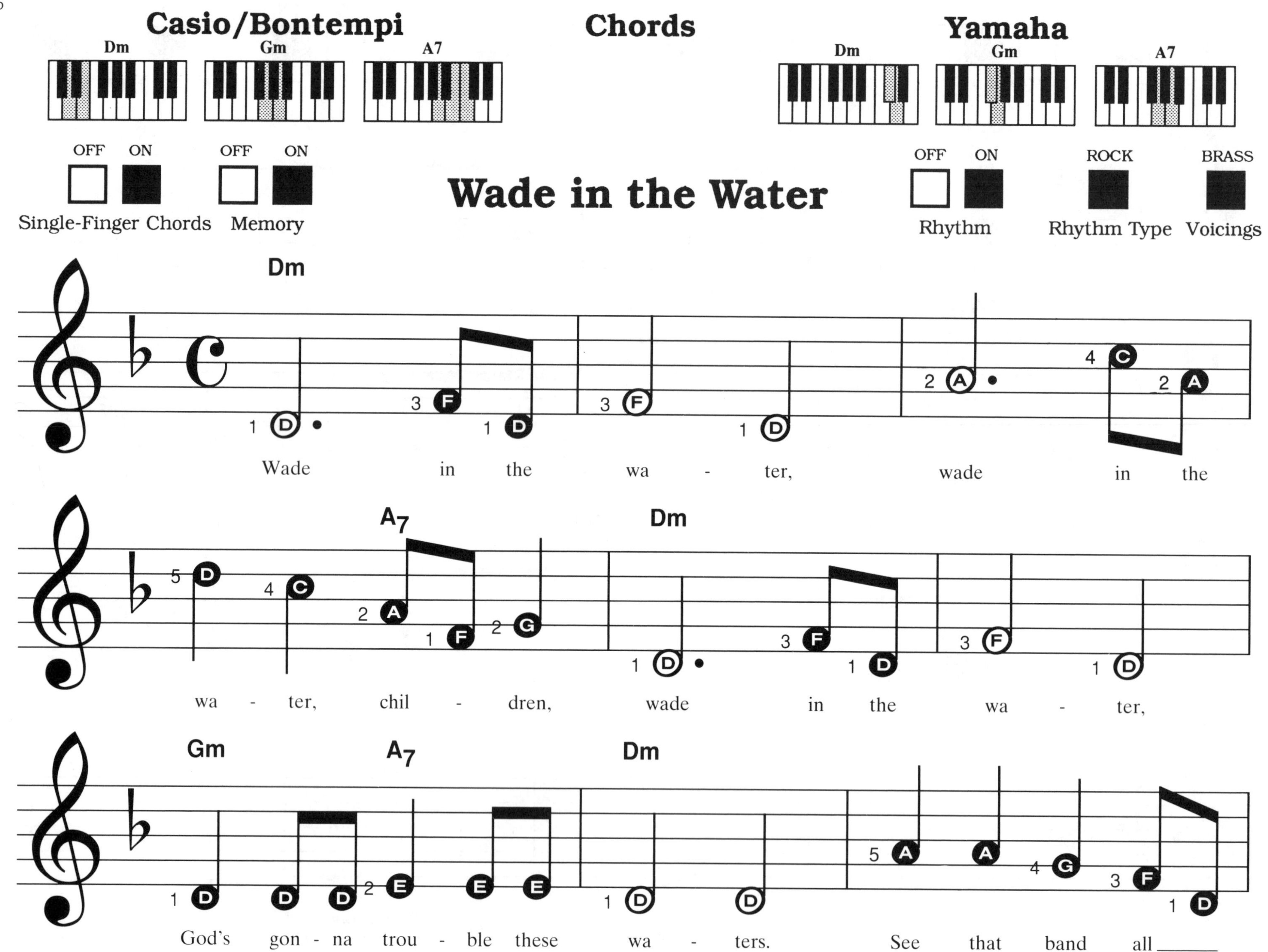
Casio/Bontempi
Dm
Gm
A7
Chords
Yamaha
Dm
Gm
A7
OFF ON
Single-Finger Chords
OFF ON
Memory
Wade in the Water
OFF ON
Rhythm
ROCK
Rhythm Type
BRASS
Voicings
Dm
Wade in the wa - ter, wade in the
A7
Dm
wa - ter, chil - dren, wade in the wa - ter,
Gm
A7
Dm
God's gon - na trou - ble these wa - ters. See that band all

A7
dressed in white? God's gon - na trou - ble these wa - ters.
Dm
Looks like a band of the Is - rael - ites!
Gm
A7
Dm
God's gon - na trou - ble these wa - ters.

Left-Hand Notes

Now we will learn to play chords and notes with the left hand. *Turn off Automatic Chords or Single-Finger Chords.* Left-hand notes are written in the bass clef.

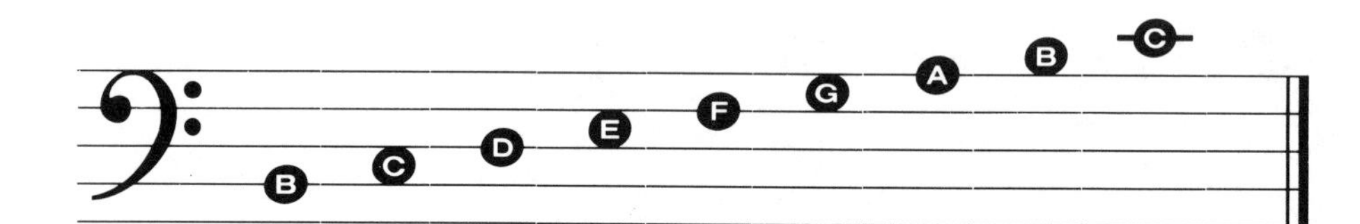

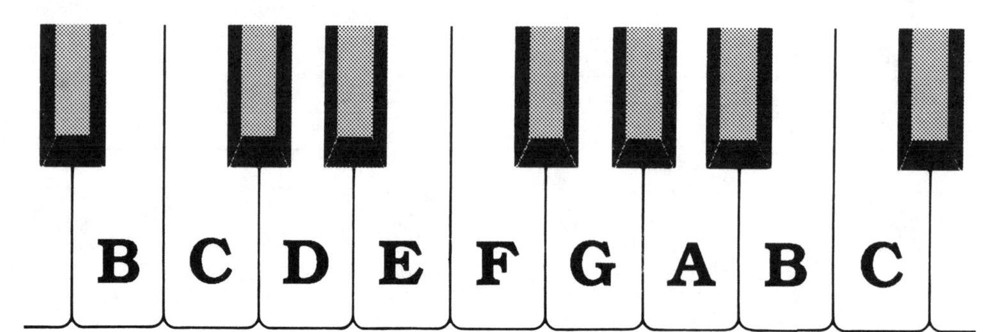

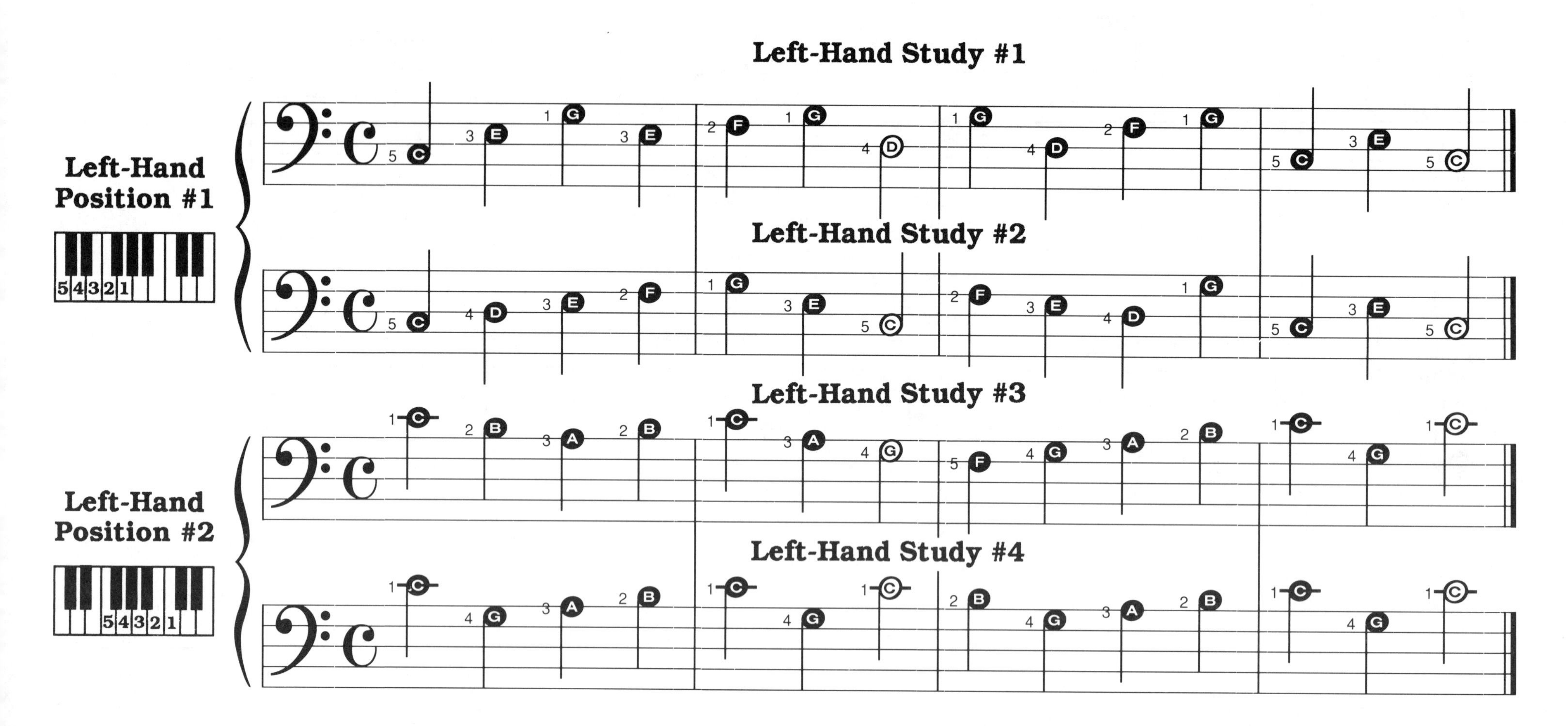

Both Hands Together

Slowly

[Practice each hand separately, then play both parts together]

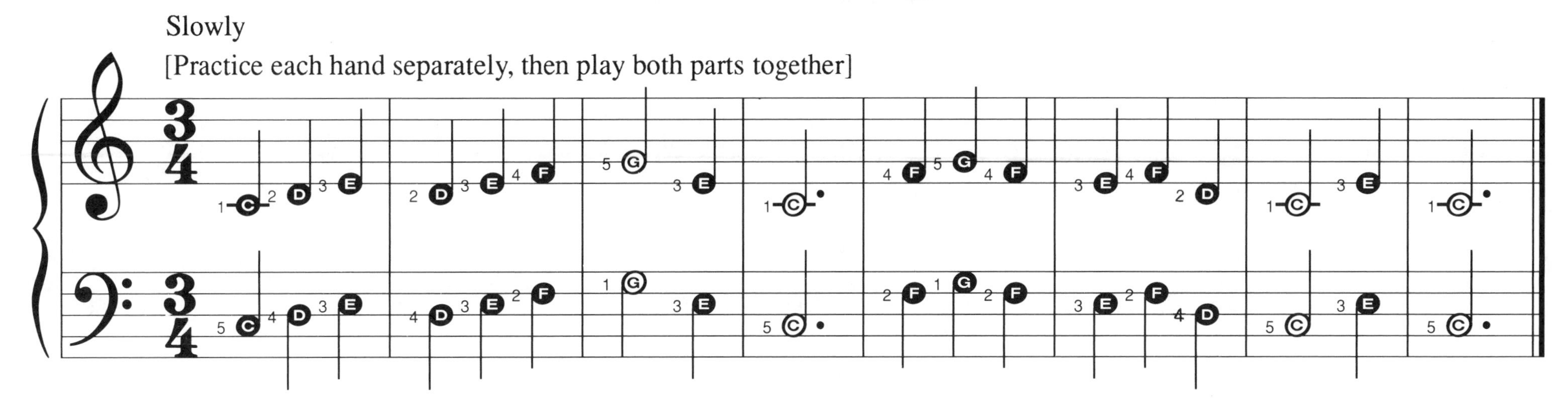

Song

[Practice each hand separately, then play both parts together]

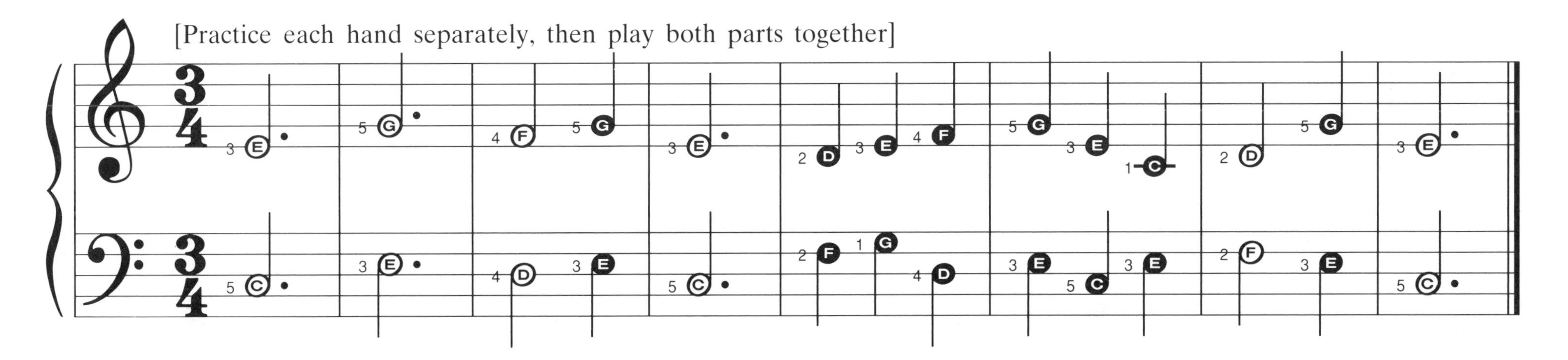

Ode to Joy

Largo

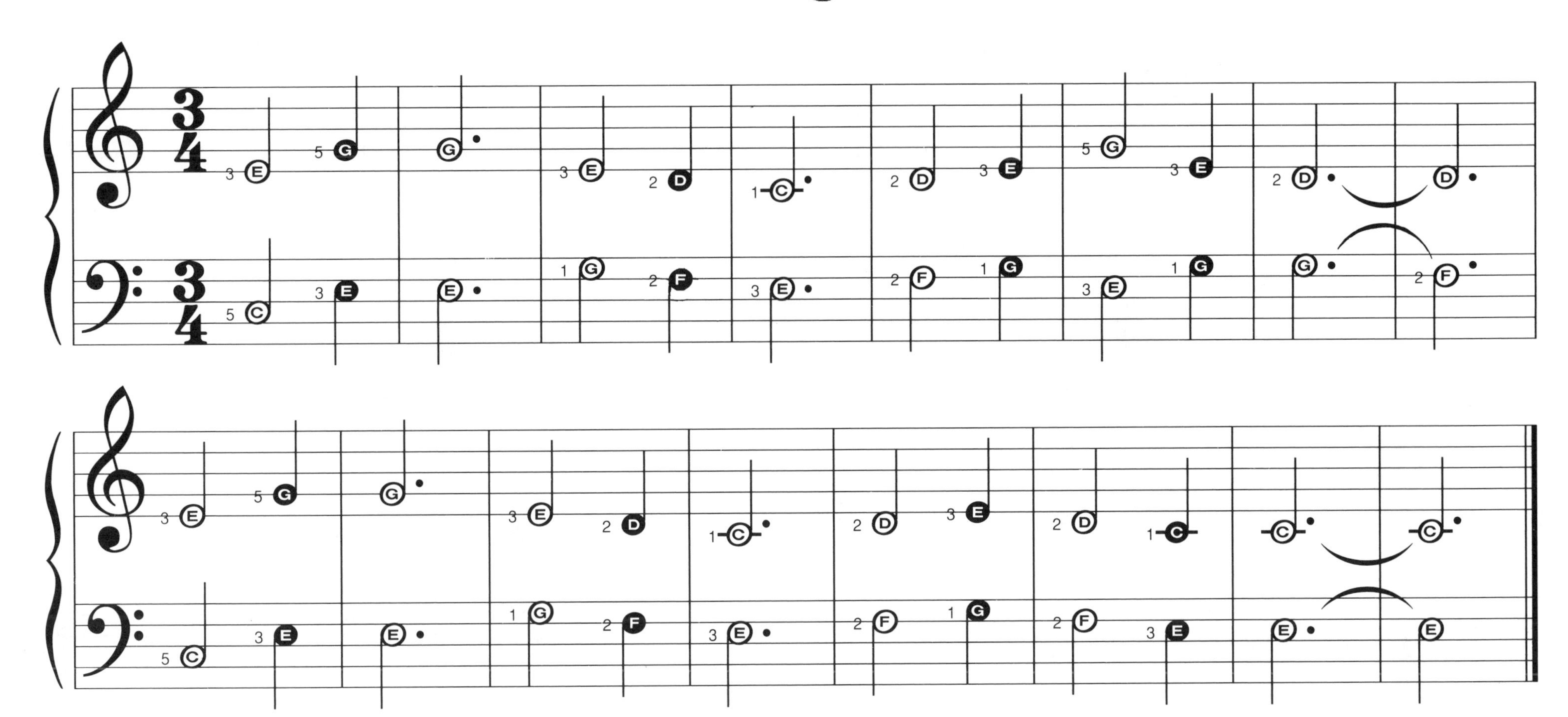

2-Part Harmony

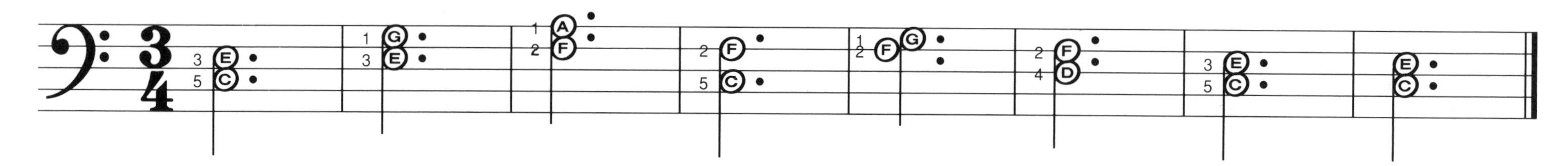

For He's a Jolly Good Fellow

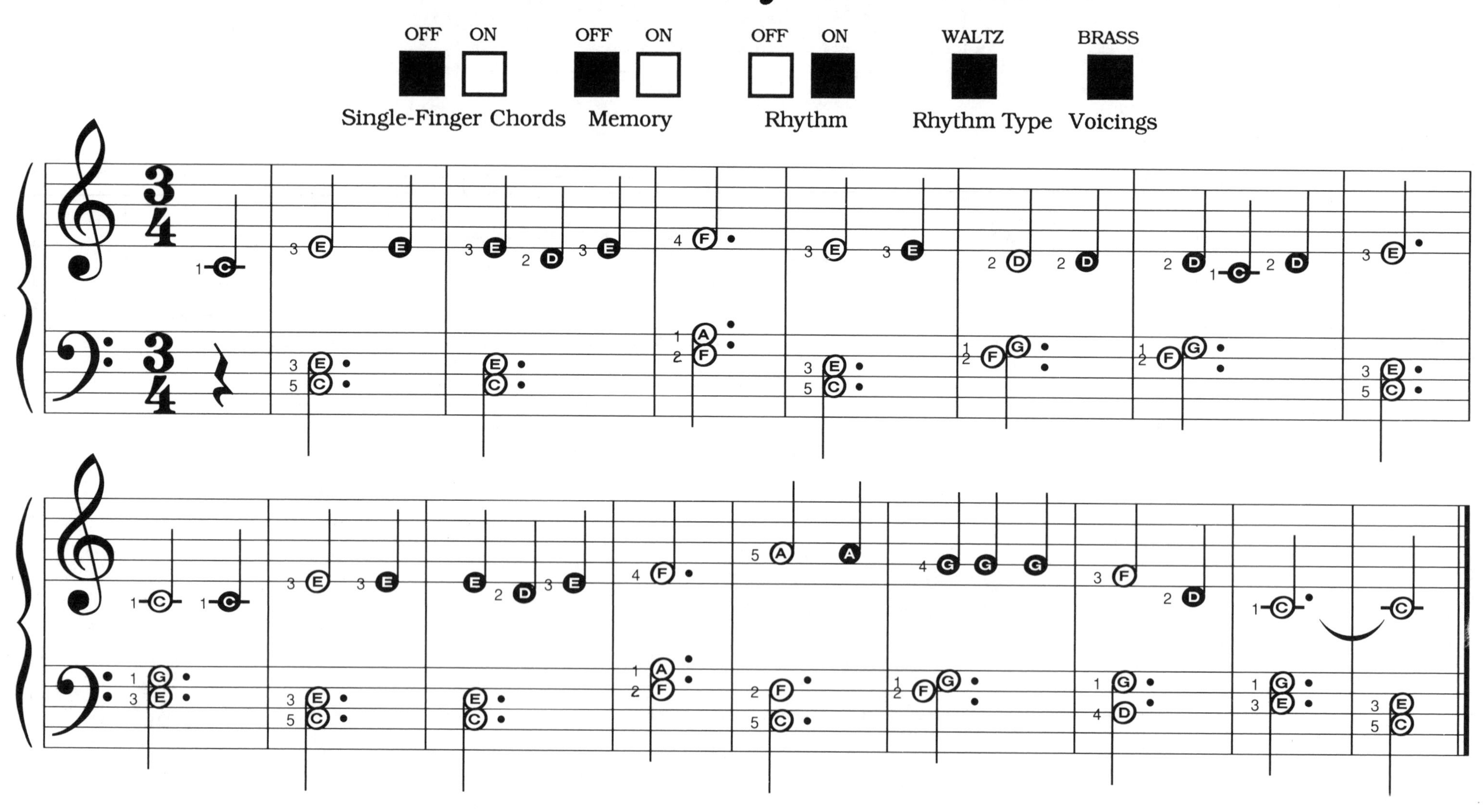

Jacob's Ladder

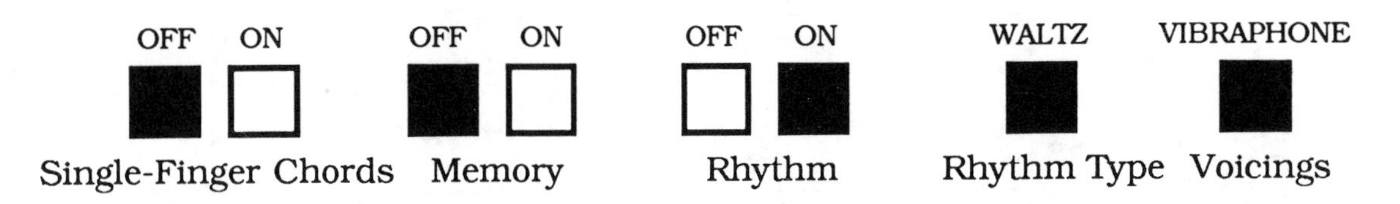

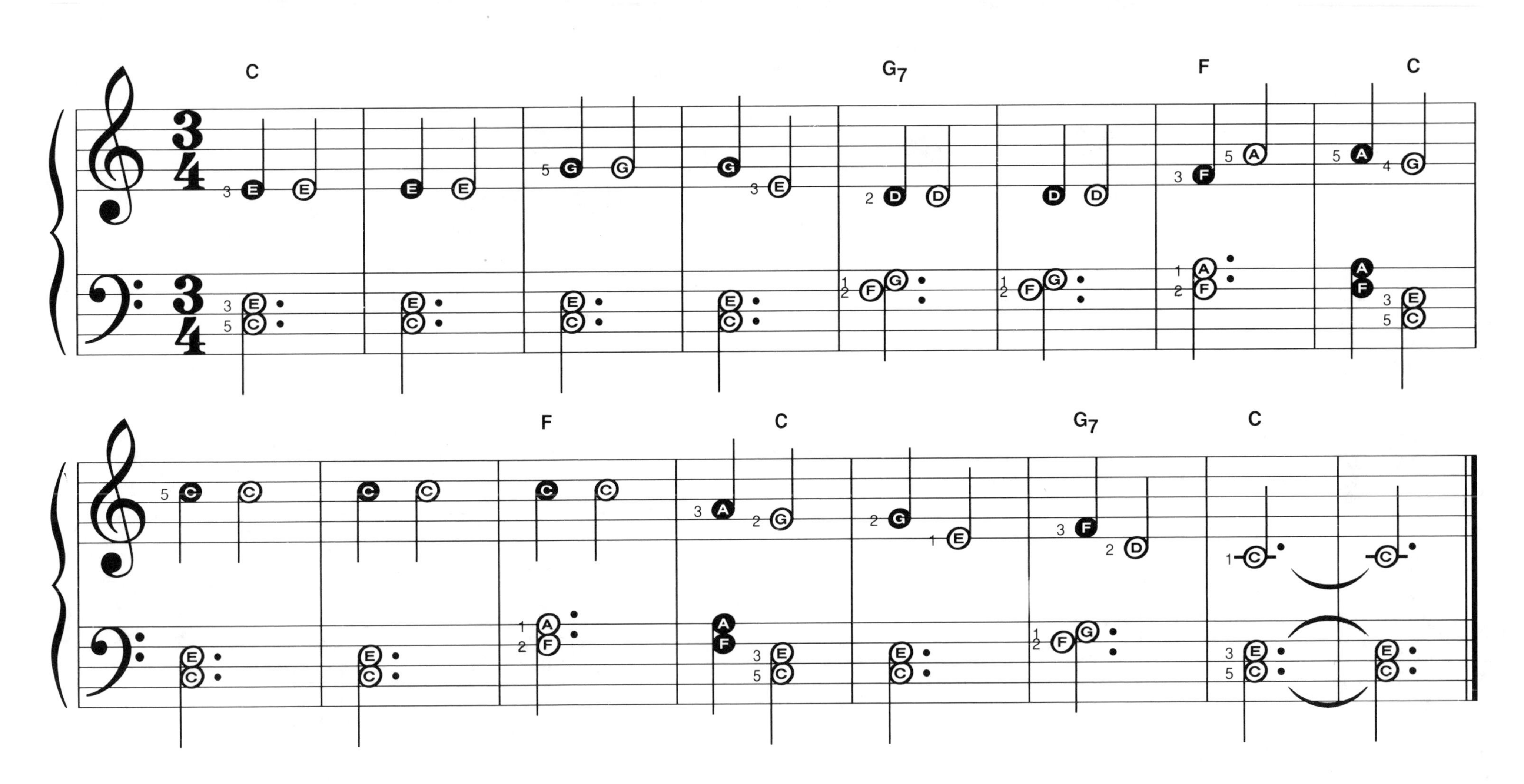

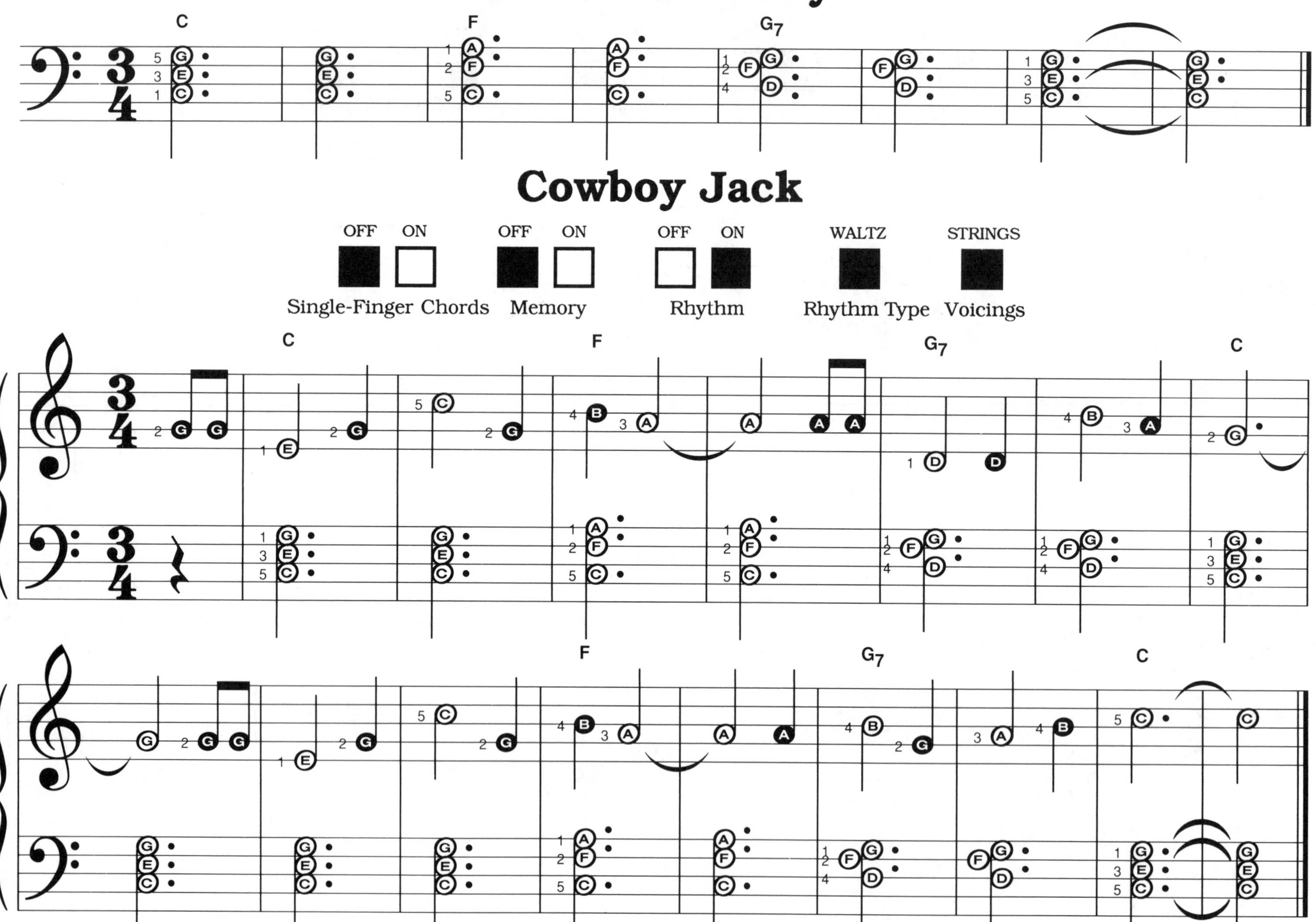
3-Part Harmony
C
F
G7
Cowboy Jack
OFF ON
Single-Finger Chords
OFF ON
Memory
OFF ON
Rhythm
WALTZ
Rhythm Type
STRINGS
Voicings

Cowboy Jack/Broken-Chord Accompaniment

Silent Night

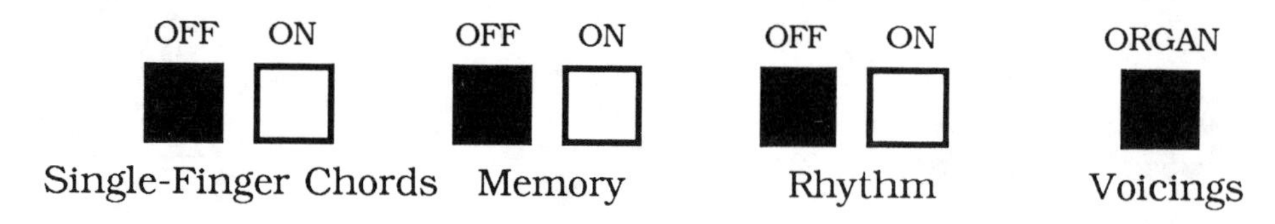

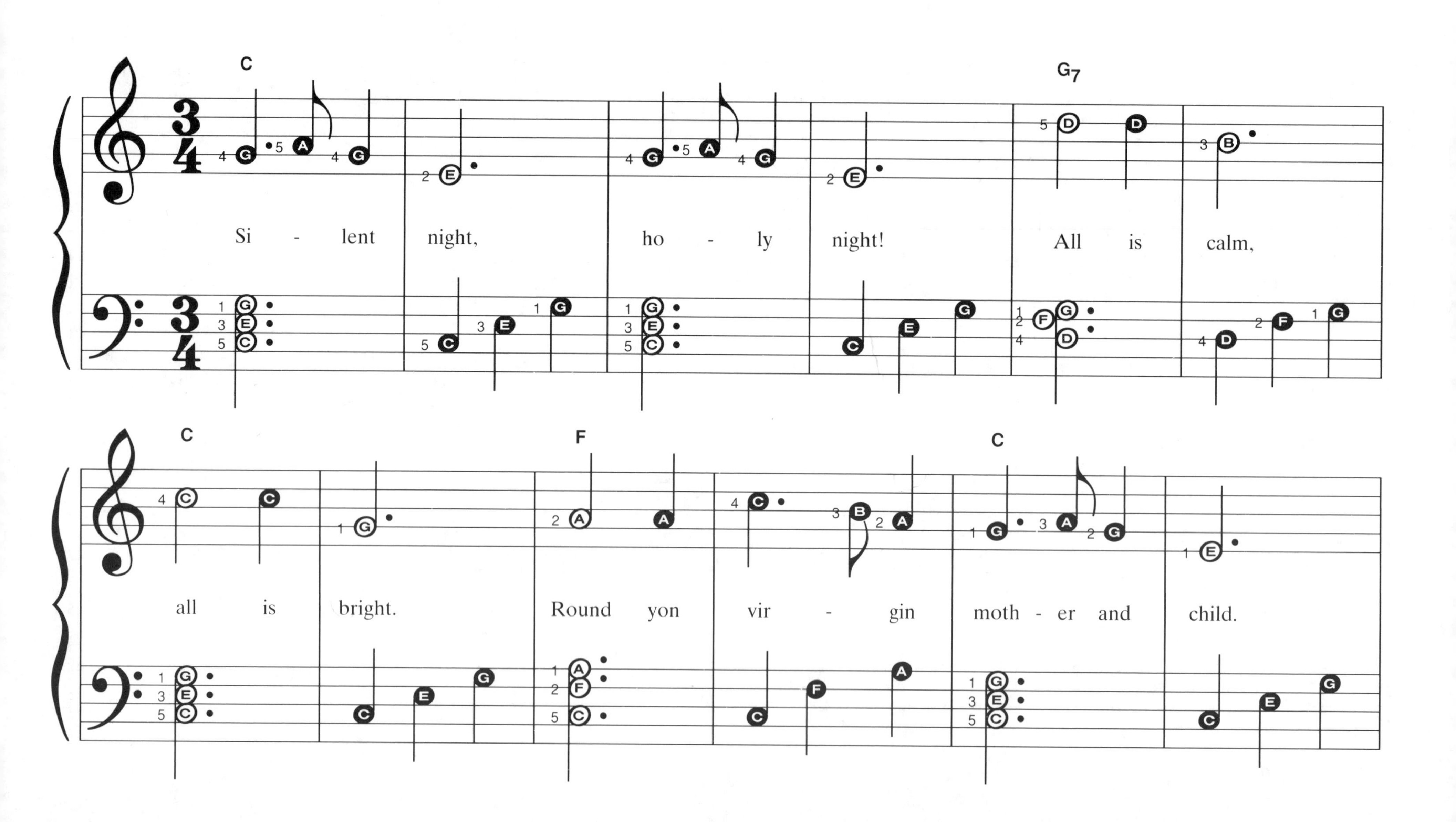

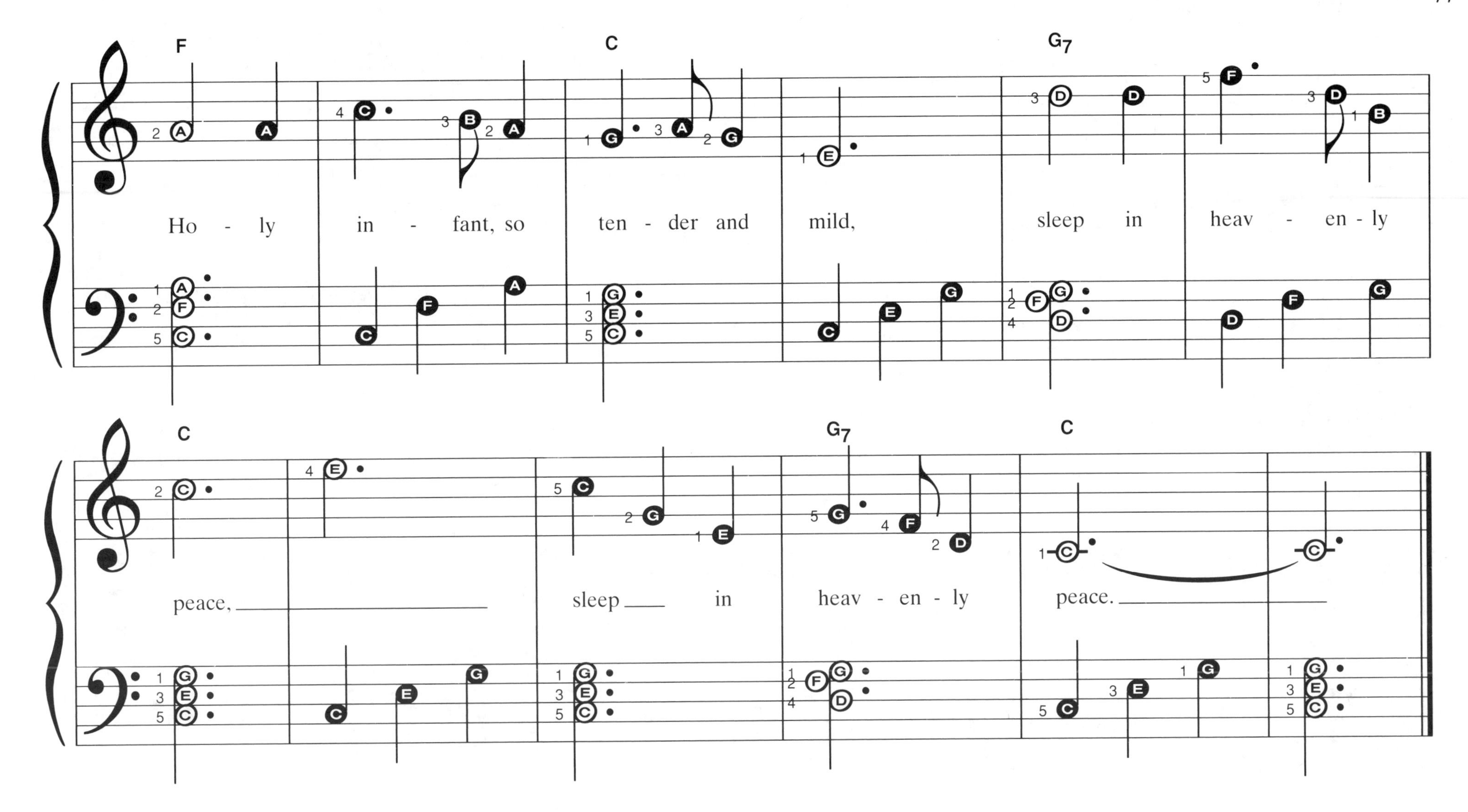
F
C
G7
Ho - ly in - fant, so ten - der and mild, sleep in heav - en - ly
C
G7
C
peace, sleep in heav - en - ly peace.

C♯ D♭ D♯ E♭ F♯ G♭ G♯ A♭ A♯ B♭ C♯ D♭ D♯ E♭ F♯ G♭ G♯ A♭ A♯ B♭ C♯ D♭ D♯ E♭ F♯ G♭ G♯ A♭ A♯ B♭ C♯ D♭ D♯ E♭ F♯ G♭ G♯ A♭ A♯ B♭

C D E F G A B C D E F G A B C D E F G A B C D E F G A B C

ACCOMPANIMENT KEYS — SOLO / MELODY KEYS

Check your owner's manual to see where the break is that divides melody keys from accompaniment keys.

ELECTRONIC KEYBOARD CHORD CHART

Remember to turn on *Automatic Accompaniment* or *Single-Finger Chords*

MAJOR CHORDS

All Keyboards

RULE: Play note with same name as chord.

C

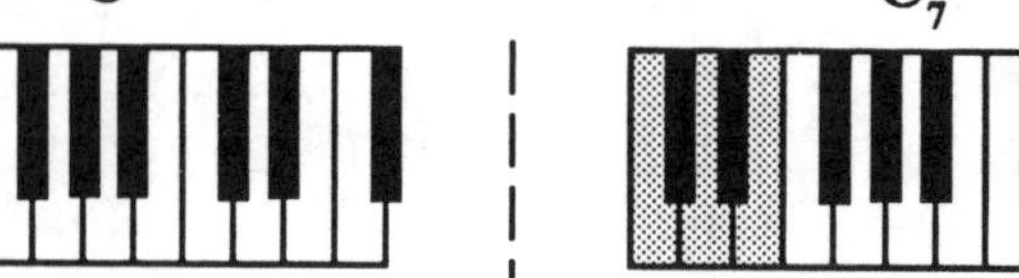

C♯ /D♭

D

D♯ / E♭

DOMINANT 7TH CHORDS

Casio / Bontempi Keyboards

RULE: Play note with same name as chord <u>and</u> play next 2 white keys to the *right* of chord note.

C_7

$C\sharp_7$ / $D\flat_7$

D_7

$D\sharp_7$ / $E\flat_7$

Yamaha Keyboards

RULE: Play note with same name as chord <u>and</u> play 1st white key to the *left* of chord note.

C_7

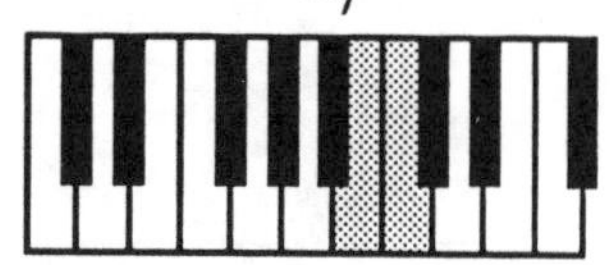

$C\sharp_7$ / $D\flat_7$

D_7

$D\sharp_7$ / $E\flat_7$

MINOR CHORDS

Casio/Bontempi Keyboards

RULE: Play note with same name as chord <u>and</u> play next white key to the *right* of the chord note.

Cm

C♯m / D♭m

Dm

D♯m / E♭m

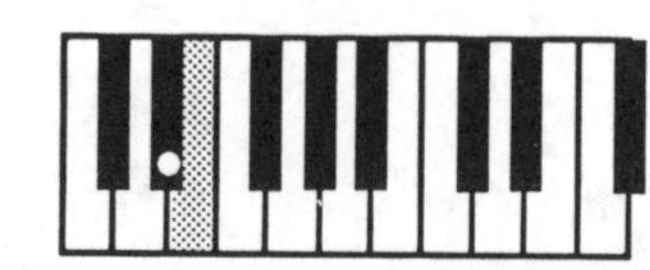

Yamaha Keyboards

RULE: Play note with same name as chord <u>and</u> play 1st black key to the *left* of the chord note.

Cm

C♯m / D♭m

Dm

D♯m / E♭m

All Keyboards

E

F

F♯ / G♭

G

G♯/ A♭

A

A♯ / B♭

B

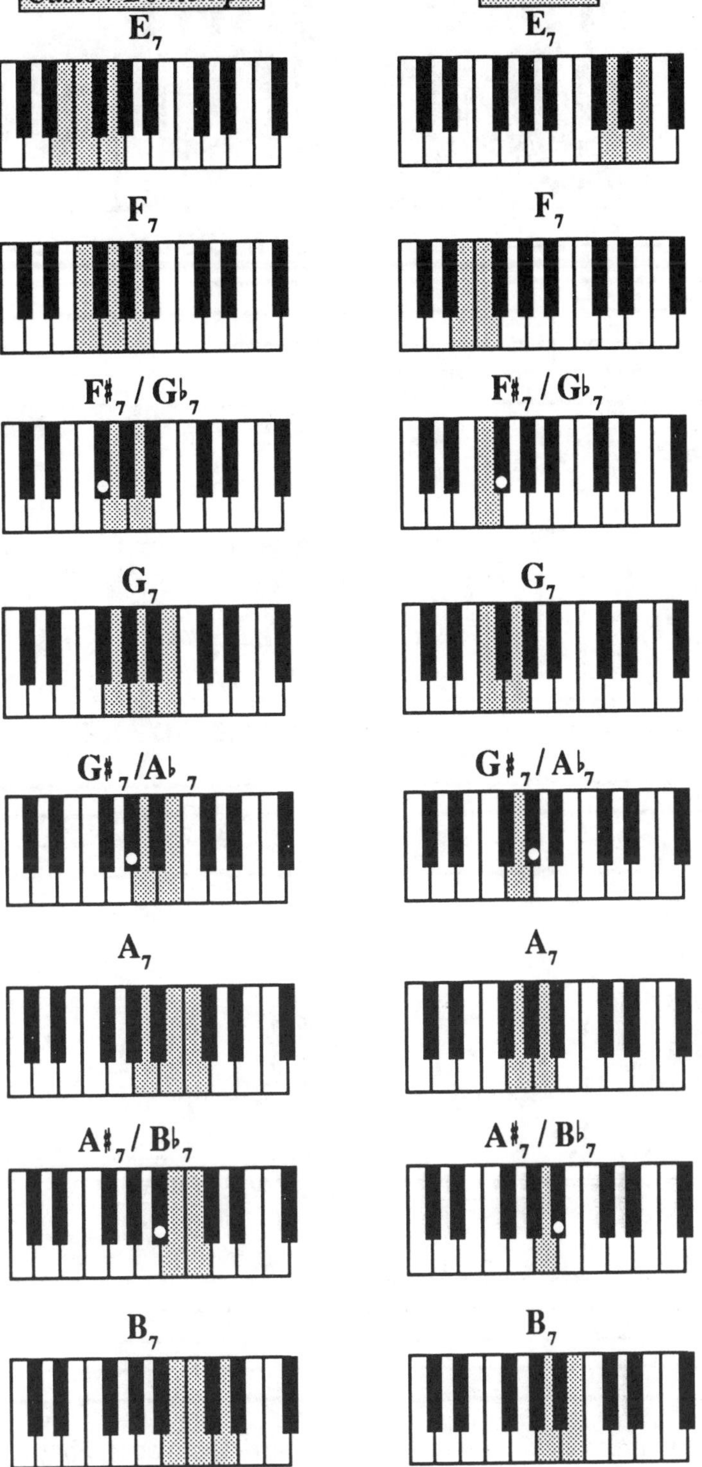

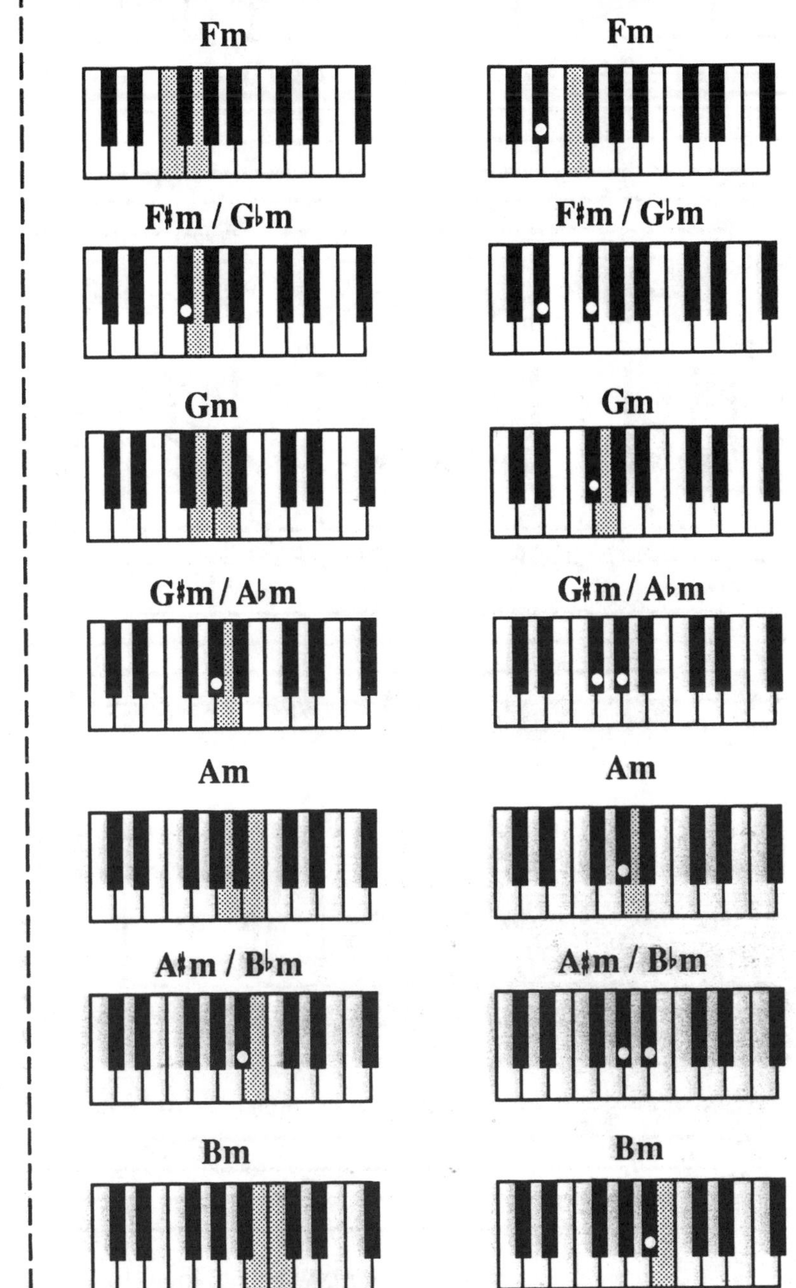

MELODY NOTE CHART*

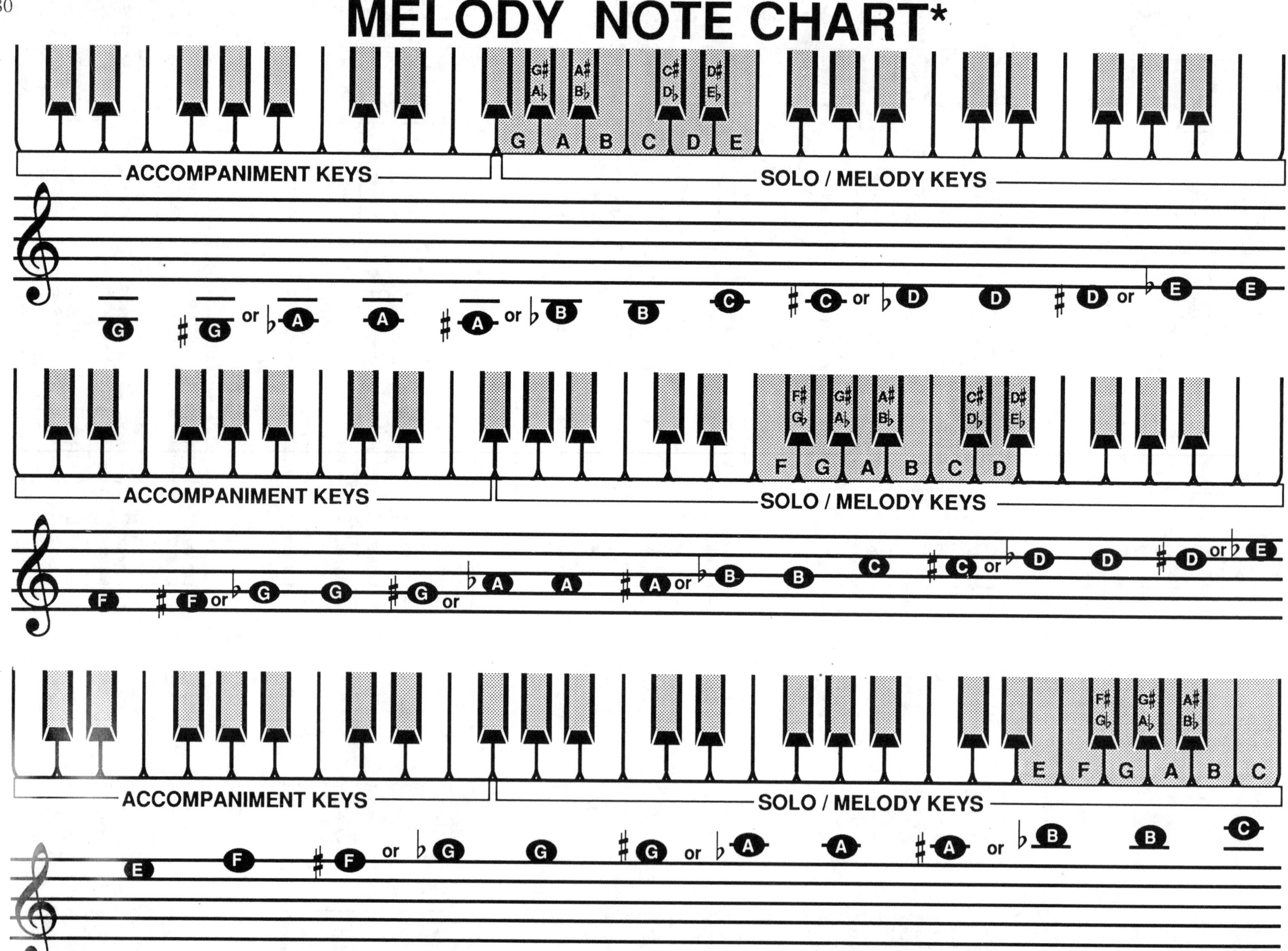

*Check your owner's manual to see where the break is that divides melody keys from accompaniment keys.